### About the author

Aidan Hegarty was born in Dungiven in Co. Derry and lives there with his wife Dorothy and two grown-up children. He was a primary school teacher near Derry for thirty years and is now retired. In 2003 he published *1969 – A Turbulent Year in Dungiven* which chronicled events in the town including the death of Francis McCloskey the first casualty of 'The Troubles'.

# JOHN MITCHEL
A Cause Too Many

# JOHN MITCHEL
A Cause Too Many

AIDAN HEGARTY

CAMLANE PRESS

## Acknowledgements

My thanks are due to Declan O'Kane who kindly allowed me access to his fine collection of related books. I would also like to thank Dominic O'Kane for all his help, encouragement and sound advice and Cathal Hasson who was only a phone call away when clarification was needed. Finally and closer to home, a special word of thanks to Dorothy for her patience and faith and Fionnuala for her valued opinion.

Thanks to M H Gill for assistance with this publication.

Published by
Camlane Press

Camlane Press
is represented in Ireland and U.K. by
Lagan Press
1A Bryson Street
Belfast BT5 4ES
Email: lagan-press@e-books.org.uk
Website: www.lagan-press.org.uk

© Aidan Hegarty 2005

The moral rights of the author have been asserted

ISBN-10: 0-9551706-0-5

ISBN-13: 978-0-9551706-0-7

Author: Aidan Hegarty
Title: John Mitchel
A Cause Too Many
2005

Set in Goudy
Printed by: J. H. Haynes & Co. Ltd

# Contents

| | | |
|---|---|---|
| *Introduction* | | 11 |
| Chapter 1 | The Early Years | *15* |
| Chapter 2 | Political Initiation | *21* |
| Chapter 3 | Mitchel Joins Repeal and the *Nation* | *25* |
| Chapter 4 | Mitchel and the Great Famine | *31* |
| Chapter 5 | No Union in Repeal | *42* |
| Chapter 6 | Mitchel on O'Connell | *46* |
| Chapter 7 | Mitchel Leaves the *Nation* and Confederation | *54* |
| Chapter 8 | The *United Irishman* | *60* |
| Chapter 9 | Trial and Transportation | *65* |
| Chapter 10 | *Jail Journal* 1848-53 | *69* |
| Chapter 11 | Young Ireland Rebellion 1848 | *76* |
| Chapter 12 | Van Diemen's Land | *81* |
| Chapter 13 | New Life in America | *87* |
| Chapter 14 | Washington and Paris | *98* |
| Chapter 15 | American Civil War 1861-65 | *102* |
| Chapter 16 | Mitchel and Fenianism | *115* |
| Chapter 17 | The *Irish Citizen* | *123* |
| Chapter 18 | Mitchel Returns in Triumph | *127* |
| Chapter 19 | Death of John Mitchel | *134* |
| Chapter 20 | The Immortal Part of Him | *138* |
| Chapter 21 | Last of the Line | *153* |
| *Selected Bibliography* | | 159 |

**Dedication**

To
Dorothy, Sean and Fionnuala
who contributed in their own individual way
to the writing of this book

# Introduction

FAMILIAR AND REVERED NAMES like Tone and Emmet, Parnell and Pearse illuminate the pages of Irish history but there are lesser known names whose contribution in shaping this nation's future was no less important. One such name is that of John Mitchel. When we hear his name we inevitably think of the fanatical Young Irelander who wrote the much acclaimed *Jail Journal* over one hundred and fifty years ago. We might also associate his name with transportation to the Australian penal colony known as Van Diemen's Land and then have difficulty recalling why exactly he had been banished from his native land. Initially, my objective in writing this short biography was to answer that question and retell Mitchel's 'Irish Story'.

However, the more I researched his life the more I realised there was a great deal of information about Mitchel which was relatively unpublished, particularly his extensive 'American Story'. Here was a controversial but heart-rending chapter in his life which I felt needed to be told in a fuller and more objective manner. It certainly forms a substantial part of the overall Mitchel biography and cannot be conveniently ignored or, as was often the case, sympathetically glossed over.

His political life, up to his trial and transportation, is recorded in most histories dealing with 19th-century Ireland but his political involvement far from ended with his exile. The life of the Newry firebrand continued to be as eventful and unpredictable as ever, often mired in controversy and in death there is a marvellous sense of poetic justice. With his devoted wife Jenny, he shared a nomadic life – on three continents no less – with more than its fair share of hardship, tragedy and personal grief.

Why, in the first instance, did I decide to research the life of Mitchel and not one of the other Young Ireland leaders? The simple answer is we share the same birthplace – the County Derry town of Dungiven – and I naturally felt a closer affinity with him. Mitchel was a Northern Presbyterian, the only one in the higher echelon of Young Ireland, and this, no doubt, added to the attraction. Why would a promising young Protestant lawyer, living a comfortable life in Co. Down, commit himself so fully to a divisive cause like Irish Nationalism? He wasn't a romantic idealist like many of his contemporaries in Young Ireland yet his uncompromising nature would ensure he paid a greater price than they.

As an additional incentive, the researching of Mitchel's life would offer the opportunity to enlighten myself on what was undoubtedly one of the most exciting periods in Irish history – Daniel O'Connell, Repeal, Young Ireland and the founding of the *Nation*. It was also the period which gave us the Great Famine, that catastrophic event, which more than anything, impacted on Mitchel's thinking and ultimately changed the entire course of his life. And through it all, there was an inevitability he seemed powerless to prevent and, in the end, he openly provoked.

In this book I have tried to cover aspects of Mitchel's personality and life the reader might not be familiar with. It must be stated at the outset that he was a more flawed character than is generally recognised but this only made him a more absorbing subject for research. His elopement to England with Jenny when she was a sixteen-year-old schoolgirl and he was a twenty-yearold solicitor's apprentice is an engaging story in itself. This impulsive streak would manifest itself at regular intervals throughout an often disordered and migrant life.

Mitchel's twenty year stay in America and close identification with the Southern Confederacy during the Civil War was a regrettable period in his life. The question this unavoidably poses for researcher and reader alike will always remain. How much should Mitchel's lesser known American history influence our overall judgement of his position in Irish history? His committed role in two basically dissimilar causes is certainly difficult to reconcile. Sadly his Confederate connection would also effect a period of immense personal sacrifice for John and Jenny Mitchel.

The extent of Mitchel's journalistic prowess and literary talents are often overlooked or at best, understated, even by his greatest admirers. Unfortunately, he was prone to using this exceptional talent to express unpopular views openly and unapologetically, a trait which often landed him in trouble. Always resolute in his beliefs, he was never one to retract or even moderate his views regardless of the consequences.

However, it is Mitchel's radical analysis and in the end, open warfare with the British Government over its 'genocidal' Famine Policy that he is probably best remembered. With ferocious intensity he defends his premise that famine was not Divine Providence visited on a dispirited, near-destitute people, but a deliberate English creation to combat an over-population crisis in Ireland. This was Mitchel in his element – the obsessive, re-invented Young Irelander of the Famine years, at war on all fronts. Friends and foes alike incurred his wrath. He may even have been at war with himself such was the passion of his rage.

I hope the reader will find this short biography of one of the most interesting and paradoxical characters in 19th-century Irish history, enjoyable as well as accessible and informative. For me it has all been an absorbing trail of discovery and a distraction in the truest sense of the word. I firmly believe that for most readers it will contain a few surprises or raise a few eyebrows. Hopefully it will also encourage further reading and open debate on Mitchel and that fascinating period in our history associated with him.

For this very reason I have written the story with the 'uninitiated historian' very much in mind. I have tried, as far as is possible, to avoid writing a routine chronicle of events in

Mitchel's life preferring to adopt a more 'human interest' slant. Similarly, it was not my intention to attempt to write a comprehensive history of mid 19th-century Ireland or, for that matter, the American Civil War. Rather, I have tried to tell the John Mitchel story as accurately as I can, giving a simple background of the political climates which prevailed at the time in Ireland and later in America.

I trust there are not too many glaring inaccuracies regarding dates, events, quotations, and personnel and that I have been fair in assessing the roles of the other prominent players, particularly within Repeal, Young Ireland and the Fenians. Above all, I hope I have presented an authentic and objective account of the life of the unrepentant rebel described by Arthur Griffith as 'The man, Nature gifted with genius'.

## Chapter 1

# The Early Years

JOHN MITCHEL, 19th-CENTURY writer, political journalist and Young Irelander, was born in the Co. Derry town of Dungiven on 3rd November 1815. His father, the Reverend John Mitchel, was a Presbyterian minister and a native of Claudy also in Co. Derry. In 1805 he was appointed minister to Camnish Parish Church situated about two miles from Dungiven. Six years later, while still serving his worthy parishioners in Dungiven the Reverend Mitchel married Mary Haslett. She was a member of a highly respected Presbyterian family from the South Derry town of Maghera. Notably, Mary's older brother William Haslett would later aspire to Mayor of Derry in 1843. He was also on the board of directors of one of the city's main banks on Shipquay Street.

Reverend Mitchel and his wife Mary had six surviving children, four girls and two boys. The eldest two children, John and Matilda, were born at Camnish Manse, Dungiven. Two sons and a daughter born to the Reverend Mitchel and his wife had died in infancy, so John, as their first surviving son, would have been very much loved. Their second son and youngest child, William, would share many of the highs and lows in his older brother's celebrated life.

The Reverend Mitchel was believed to be sympathetic to the ideals of the Society of United Irishmen founded by Wolfe Tone. (In a speech delivered by his son John in Conciliation Hall in 1848, Mitchel asserts that his father was in fact, a member of that society but there is no real evidence of this.) The original aims of the Society, formed in 1791, were equality for all religious groupings in Ireland and a radical reform of the Irish Parliament which was totally unrepresentative and controlled by England. Catholics didn't have a vote even let alone sit in the Dublin parliament at that time.

However, under the influence of Wolfe Tone, the Society would soon become completely republican/separatist in outlook, hoping to 'break all connection with England ... and to substitute the common name of Irishman in place of the denominations of Protestant, Catholic and Dissenter'. The majority of the Society's membership in the north of the country – based largely in Counties Antrim and Down – was of the Presbyterian faith. Leaders in Ulster like Henry Monroe in Down and Henry Joy McCracken in Antrim, both executed in 1798, were Presbyterians.

In 1819 the Mitchel family moved to Derry when the Reverend Mitchel took up a larger ministry in the city. He served in First Derry Presbyterian Church for four years, before moving to Newry in 1823. In his letter of resignation to the Church authorities in Derry, the Reverend Mitchel explained that he preferred a single ministry – in Derry he shared his ministry with the Reverend George Hay – and Newry offered him this opportunity. John Mitchel was seven years old when the family moved to Newry.

In their comfortable home, 'Dromolane House' situated outside the town, John spent seven happy years attending the school of Dr Henderson where he excelled in the Classics and English. It was while at school in Newry he first met John Martin from nearby Loughhorne who would be his most 'staunch and worthy' companion throughout his life. John Martin was three years older than Mitchel and was of a more serious nature but they were to become closer than brothers and their lives would be inextricably linked to their very deaths. Both men were avid readers, shared similar tastes in books, and were outstanding linguists and classical scholars. Mitchel later described John Martin in his *Jail Journal* as 'simply the best, worthiest, and most thoroughly high-minded man I ever knew'. At aged just fifteen John Mitchel had moved to Trinity College, Dublin to continue his studies. John Martin enrolled at Trinity about the same time to study medicine.

Mitchel's biographer, Louis J Walsh, describes him as 'a boy, who from his earliest years had an extraordinary feel for natural beauties especially for mountains and streams. Often he would go for long solitary rambles through the hills and was out long into the night. He knew every mountain, stream and glen within walking distance of Newry, and to the last day of his life the sight and names of them were fresh in his memory.'

In an entry in *Jail Journal* written while on his long, exhausting voyage into exile, Mitchel vividly recalls his childhood in Dungiven and Newry:

> and my ear and brain are filled with the murmurings of the Rivers Roe and Bann.

In another lyrical entry in *Jail Journal* dated 13th September 1848 he writes:

> Well known to me by day and by night are the voices of Ireland's winds and waters, the faces of her ancient mountains. I see it, I hear it all – for by the wondrous power of imagination, informed by strong love, I do indeed live more truly in Ireland than on these unblessed rocks.

These lines were written as a wistful Mitchel sat on a rocky pier in Bermuda and gazed out upon 'that immeasurable boundless blue' of the Atlantic Ocean. He concludes the entry on an even more nostalgic note:

> But what avails it? Do my eyes strain over the sea in vain? My soul yearn in vain? Has not the Queen of England banished me from the land where my mother bore me, where my father's bones are laid?

In 1834, Mitchel graduated from Trinity College with a Bachelor of Arts degree. The fact he was still only eighteen years old gives us a clear indication how exceptionally gifted a student he was. Interestingly, the name of John Mitchel was later removed from the list of graduates for that year, 1834. The Trinity Academia, with its strong Ascendancy background, was obviously not too impressed by its young prodigy's later 'notoriety' and the direction his life would lead politically.

To his father's disappointment but not surprise, John decided that a life in the Ministry of the Church was not for him and a career in banking was agreed upon. This would prove a brief flirtation and he soon discovered that, like the church, the world of finance was definitely not for him either. His greatest difficulty now was explaining his decision to quit banking to his father as he felt he had once again, let him down.

Nevertheless, he left Derry and his Uncle William Haslett after only a few weeks and returned home to Newry. A humdrum occupation, chained to a desk, totting up meaningless figures and filling ledgers, was just not suited to someone of Mitchel's restless temperament. In a letter, written to his father before he left Derry, he described banking as 'a thing that is really not fit for me, nor I for it'. In the same letter he writes of the long working hours as 'unremitting slavery'.

William Haslett was believed to be a hard taskmaster and this may have been a contributory factor in the young Mitchel wishing to break free. Again in correspondence with his father he wrote that banking 'would not only require an utter sacrifice of all my habits and inclinations, but would preclude all sorts of reading, even I think for college.' This was undoubtedly a major consideration and too great a sacrifice for someone with a voracious appetite for books like Mitchel.

Shortly after his return from Derry, John announced his engagement to a girl from Belfast six years older than himself. Her name was Ann and her family seem to have been known personally to Jenny Mitchel's family. John had just turned nineteen and, not surprisingly, his parents voiced their opposition to an early marriage. Ann's parents accepted the Reverend Mitchel's ruling and refused to allow any further liaison between the young couple. John at first was heart-broken but, time being the great healer – and it did take some considerable time and long solitary walks in the Mournes – he was eventually able to put the thwarted love affair behind him.

This was to be the first example of that impulsive nature which would be evident, time and time again, throughout his life.

After his brief encounter with the world of banking, Mitchel's next consideration was a career in law and he joined the law firm of John Quinn of Newry and Dublin as a solicitor's apprentice. In the spring of 1836 he met Jenny Verner, the only daughter of a British military officer and was immediately captivated by her. Mitchel was only twenty years old and Jenny sixteen. She was still a schoolgirl and was attending Miss Bryden's Finishing School in Newry. It was a very select school where young ladies were prepared to take their place in 'fashionable' society. Not surprisingly their courtship was very much a secretive liaison as it didn't meet with the approval of Jenny's parents.

Captain James Verner's objections were twofold. Firstly, he considered his daughter was much too young for a serious relationship, and secondly, he didn't believe a solicitor's apprentice was financially capable of supporting his only daughter. Of greater significance, as the niece of Colonel Sir William Verner, MP for Armagh, Jenny was probably believed to be of a much higher social standing than the son of a Presbyterian clergyman.

The situation grew so intolerable that the hapless couple were forced to elope to Liverpool but were brought back to Newry by Jenny's parents only days before they were due to be married. Less than a year after their first meeting, John Mitchel and his young bride Jenny Verner were married on 3rd February 1837. The service was held at Drumcree Parish Church, Portadown in Co. Armagh. (Another source claims the marriage took place at the parish church in Dromore, Co Down.) The Verners were a wealthy, landed family from Loughgall, approximately seven miles from Portadown, so Drumcree Church is the more probable location for the wedding.

There is no record of how Captain Verner and his wife accepted this union but Jenny was warmly welcomed into the Mitchel family which she soon looked upon as her own. Jenny's parents died some ten years after their daughter's marriage but according to Jenny's biographer, Rebecca O'Conner, they became reconciled with their daughter shortly before their deaths. We can only assume that Jenny's Uncle William, a leader in the loyal Orange Order and local magistrate may not have been quite so forgiving. John Mitchel had done little in the interim to endear himself to the local Conservative MP and the owner of land in three different counties.

After a brief honeymoon in Dublin, John and Jenny set up home in Newry, in a modest house near his parents' home in the townland of Dromolane. Little over a year later Jenny gave birth to their first son whom they named John. Mitchel later modestly admitted that his son had been named after him, then quickly added, 'but more after his grandfather'. Like the Reverend Mitchel before him, John Mitchel would be father to six children, three sons and three daughters.

Meanwhile Mitchel continued to work with Quinn's Solicitors but was still unsure if he had chosen the right profession. Rather, he saw it as an economic necessity now that he was both a husband and a father. He did, however, persevere and became a very capable legal apprentice, painstaking in all his paperwork. To alleviate the pressure of his day work he joined a Newry literary society in the evenings. It was here that he renewed his great passion for writing, which was now becoming more and more of a historical and political nature.

## Chapter 2

# Political Initiation

IT WAS THROUGH HIS legal experiences that Mitchel's awareness of political injustice mainly developed. A frequent visitor to the law courts, he saw at first hand that religious discrimination was still commonplace despite the Catholic Emancipation Act of 1829 and that the law was still stacked against landless Catholics. The Act, granted reluctantly by the Westminster Parliament and due largely to the efforts of Daniel O'Connell, meant that Catholics could now hold government office and sit in the British Parliament. The Oath of Supremacy of 1536 – recognition of the English monarch as head of the Church in Ireland as well as Britain – was particularly abhorrent to Catholics. Under the Emancipation Act it was replaced by the less offensive Oath of Allegiance to the English monarch.

However, it was some years before the government actually gave positions to Catholics even if they were prepared to recognise the Oath of Allegiance. It did mean they could enter Parliament with immediate effect and Daniel O'Connell finally took his seat in the House of Commons the following year, 1830. He had been successfully elected in Co. Clare in June 1828 but was debarred because he refused to take the Oath of Supremacy. He stood again in a by-election in 1830 and won the seat convincingly, defeating the Conservative candidate, a local landlord named Vesey Fitzgerald.

O'Connell was a candidate for the Catholic Association which he had founded with Richard Lalor Sheil in 1823. Both men were lawyers and they took great care to keep the association within the law. O'Connell had the distinction of becoming the first Irish Catholic MP to enter Westminster. With his tall, burly figure and powers of oratory he was a formidable proponent for Irish rights and his prowess as a parliamentarian soon became evident. His seventeen years tenure as the elected member for Co. Clare would neither be dull nor uneventful. It was a measure of O'Connell's popularity at the time that, in the General Election of 1832, forty five of the one hundred and five MPs were his supporters – Repeal MPs

Twelve years after the Emancipation Act, judges and court officials were still manifestly prejudiced and this outraged Mitchel's sense of justice. He saw at first hand that Catholics still had many legitimate grievances that must be addressed. Catholic Emancipation offered nothing to the poor in Ireland. Rents remained extremely high and most Catholics had lost their right to vote. After the Emancipation Act only freeholders paying at least £10 per year retained the vote whereas before the Act it was £2. The system of paying tithes i.e. one tenth of farm produce, to the Established Church namely the Church of Ireland also remained. The 'tithe system' still existed despite the fact that the overwhelming majority of the population at the time was Catholic.

In 1839 Daniel O'Connell, now leader of a large group of Irish MPs at Westminster and something of a national hero, was invited to attend a banquet in Newry as principal guest and speaker. The dinner had been organised by a number of influential Catholics who admired O'Connell's leadership qualities and oratorical skills in Parliament. O'Connell had never been so far north before, and Newry at that time had a strong Orange base. The invitation to O'Connell, therefore, was highly controversial and was even branded as provocative by many Protestants.

Mitchel aligned himself with the Catholic organisers. Firstly, because he was a great admirer of 'The Liberator' and his role in parliament, and, secondly, because he believed it was O'Connell's right, as leader of the majority of the Irish people to speak anywhere in Ireland. Furthermore, he believed that the Orange Institution should not be allowed to put a veto on where O'Connell could speak if people wished to hear him.

The guest speaker, however, proved a major disappointment to the more patriotic present. They had anticipated a rousing cry for Ireland's claim to nationhood and a belligerent attack on British government policy towards Ireland. Instead they were roundly treated to an appeal for patience, and reforms would be won from Lord Melbourne's Whig government. This wasn't quite what Mitchel had expected to hear either but he had taken his first tentative step into the realm of Irish politics. He would see a lot more of O'Connell in the coming years and the rapport between the two would turn increasingly antagonistic.

In February of the following year, 1840, the Reverend Mitchel died aged fifty-eight. His death was a hammer-blow for Mitchel who loved him deeply and held him in the highest esteem. His grief was intensified by acute remorse that he had caused his father unnecessary anxiety by often disregarding his wishes. He also felt that he hadn't fulfilled his true potential in his father's eyes and disappointed him by not taking up a ministry in the church. His father might have been slightly concerned at the direction his son's life was taking but there is no evidence that he voiced any criticism or even displeasure.

A decade later in his *Jail Journal*, Mitchel wrote tenderly and with some regret of his relationship with his father. He states, 'I wish the mild shade of my father wore a less reproachful aspect – and I wish he had less reason'. Written so many years after his father's death, yet he still seemed to believe that he fell some way short of his father's expectations and that his life had gone in a direction his father would not have approved of. He was, at that time, facing a period of great uncertainty and upheaval in his own life and this surely contributed to these feelings of remorse and despondency.

In June 1839 Mitchel completed his law apprenticeship and was sworn in as a barrister. He entered into partnership with a Mr. Frazer and went to take charge of a branch office in

Charles Gavan Duffy

Banbridge, Co. Down where he lived for the next six years. In the autumn of that year, 1839, he first met Charles Gavan Duffy, a chance meeting which would have far reaching consequences.

Gavan Duffy was a young journalist who hailed from Monaghan town. Although only twenty-four years old, Duffy had vast experience in journalism both in Belfast and Dublin. In Belfast he had recently taken over editorship of the popular Catholic weekly *Belfast Vindicator* and of which he would later become owner. Little did Mitchel realise at the time how influential the young, ambitious Monaghan journalist would become in shaping his future life.

## Chapter 3

# Mitchel Joins Repeal and the *Nation*

UNDER THE 'ACT OF Union of Britain and Ireland' of 1801, Ireland was ruled directly from Westminster. The Irish Parliament, which had existed for five hundred years, was abolished and all laws governing Ireland were made in the Parliament at Westminster. Ireland sent one hundred MPs to this 'United Kingdom Parliament' and a new era in British/Irish history had begun. For the first time a new flag, the Union Jack, flew on public buildings in Ireland. The Irish MPs were all Protestants and were drawn mainly from the wealthy landlord class. They were all pro-Union and, in most matters, supported the Conservative Party.

In 1841, Sir Robert Peel and his Conservative Party were returned to power in Westminster with a huge majority. This would mean sweeping change in British government attitude to Ireland. As Home Secretary in 1829, Peel had strongly opposed the granting of Catholic Emancipation and twelve years later, his position on Ireland hadn't changed. Daniel O'Connell realised that there was little chance reform could now be won with his bitter opponent Peel as Prime Minister. O'Connell felt that with a Whig government in power some progress could be made on reform but under Peel all hope evaporated. The Irish would continue to be treated as second class citizens within the Union so O'Connell began a new campaign of agitation. He now had one fundamental demand – the repeal of the discriminatory Act of Union which joined Ireland to Britain.

He formed what was called the Repeal Association and collected Repeal Rent, or the 'O'Connell Tribute', as it was popularly known, to cover his expenses. He had given up a very successful legal practice so this was his only source of income. The Rent was a penny per month or a shilling per year and at its peak brought in over £1000 per month. O'Connell travelled the country addressing public meetings and recruiting thousands into the association.

O'Connell hoped to win Repeal in the same way he had won Emancipation. He believed that by mobilising a mass movement of the people to peacefully demand change the government would be forced to rescind the Act of Union. At first support for Repeal was small but, due largely to the tireless work of its leader, it quickly gained momentum. O'Connell's demand was now unambiguous – only an Irish Parliament, sitting in Dublin, could solve Irish problems and best serve Irish needs. Reform was no longer an option and only the revoking of the undemocratic Act of Union would now be acceptable.

In 1842 the movement was joined by a number of young, intellectual idealists of middle-class background. One was Thomas Davis, a 28 year old Protestant barrister from Mallow in Co. Cork. He was the posthumous son of a British Army surgeon who was serving with a regiment stationed in Mallow and his mother was a native of Co. Cork. (Davis's father had died in 1814, en route to the Napoleonic wars.) Davis, like Mitchel, was a barrister and had been called to the Bar in 1838. While studying at Trinity College he became friendly with John Blake Dillon from Co. Mayo who was also a law student. They were both members of the Historical Society at Trinity, shared a deep interest in Irish politics, and had a passionate love for Ireland.

Later that year, Davis and Blake Dillon were to meet Charles Gavan Duffy, and they immediately discovered a common bond. All three supported the lobby for Repeal and greatly admired O'Connell but they wanted to go further. They believed that the Irish people needed to be educated for eventual independence from Britain. On a crisp autumn day they sat in Phoenix Park and discussed how this could best be achieved. The outcome of their conversation was the appearance on

Saturday, 18th October, 1842 of a new weekly newspaper, the *Nation*. From such humble origins began what was perhaps the most remarkable venture in the history of Irish journalism. The paper was owned by Gavan Duffy, Davis became its first editor, and all three contributed a variety of articles to it.

In a few short months the *Nation* had caught the imagination of the country in a way no other paper had ever done with its freshness and vigour. It had a weekly circulation of almost eleven thousand copies making it the largest circulation of any weekly paper in Ireland in its day. The paper contained sixteen pages of closely-printed news items, letters, and features including poems, songs and short stories. It cost 6d (2p today) which was the average daily wage of a labourer and because of its price only the well-off could afford to buy it. The reading aloud of the *Nation* by the local schoolmaster or priest soon became a feature in every chapel yard before or after Sunday Mass. In this way the message of the *Nation* reached a much greater audience.

For the first time in history an Irish paper was attracting the attention of readers outside of Ireland. When the

John Blake Dillon

French democrats founded their party newspaper they called it 'La Nation' and publicised the fact that they sought to emulate the *Nation* of Ireland. Several versions of the *Nation* appeared in America all said to be inspired by their Irish equivalent. The staunchly pro-Conservative paper, the *Dublin Warder* described the *Nation* as 'the most ominous and formidable phenomenon of these strange and menacing times.'

The *Nation* urged its readers to forget past religious and class differences and to unite to seek total independence from Britain. Irish Nationalism, as advocated by Davis, was something which would 'inflame and purify the Irish people with a lofty and heroic love of country.' There was one serious drawback however. A large section of the population, especially in the large Irish-speaking districts, was denied access to its message because the paper was written entirely in English.

An elderly judge named Plunkett, when asked at the time, 'What is the tone of 'The *Nation*?' replied, 'The tone of the *Nation* is, I believe, the tone of Wolfe Tone.' Perhaps his position as a judge explains his exaggerated opinion of its political tenor but, for the first time, Wolfe Tone and the United Irishmen of '98 were spoken of as heroes to be admired and emulated. It did, however, advocate Repeal of the Union and not total separatism as the viable political objective.

In the leading article in the very first issue dated 18th October 1842, Gavan Duffy spelt out the tone of the *Nation* in unmistakable terms. He wrote:

> With all the nicknames that serve to delude and divide us – with all the Orangemen and Ribbonmen, Torymen and Whigmen, Ultras and Moderados, and Heaven knows what rubbish besides – there are, in truth, but two parties in Ireland – those who suffer through her national degradation and those who profit by it ... That is the first article of our political creed.

Frequent articles on Irish history appeared not only to educate, but also to instil a sense of patriotism and national pride. In addition to encouraging a pride in the past, the *Nation* urged preparation for a future free from British domination. Editorials regularly called on the readership to support Irish industry by buying Irish-made goods. The *Nation* specifically campaigned to have a law passed to protect tenants against eviction and appealed to landlords to show compassion and respect the rights of their tenants. All the time, under Gavan Duffy's watchful eye, and Thomas Davis' editorship, the contents of the *Nation* were kept safely within publication laws and nothing which might be interpreted as seditious was printed.

Around this time John Mitchel's defence of Catholic victims of injustice in northern law courts was attracting the attention of the editorial staff of the *Nation*. Legal business often took Mitchel to Dublin and on one auspicious occasion he decided to call on his friend Gavan Duffy. It was then that he was first introduced to Thomas Davis who was familiar with Mitchel's reputation as a lawyer but more significantly, as a writer.

Not long after their meeting in Dublin, Duffy and Davis invited Mitchel to contribute to the very popular 'Library of Ireland' section in the *Nation*. He was reluctant at first but agreed to write, in serial form, the history of his hero Hugh O'Neill, second Earl of Tyrone. This was later published in book form as *The Life of Hugh O'Neill* and to this day is considered by many historians to be the definitive biography of the 'Great O' Neill' who was forced to flee Ireland in 1607. He died in Rome in 1616.

Now that he was gaining something of a reputation as a writer within the *Nation* it was only a matter of time before Mitchel was asked to join the Repeal Association. Proposed by Gavan Duffy and seconded by O'Connell himself, he was welcomed into the movement in 1843. Repeal was at the height of its popularity at this time and was attracting a number of Northern Protestants. As an enthusiastic member of Repeal, Mitchel's writing in the *Nation* would soon move on from the historical to the political, fuelled by the social deprivation and injustice he saw in his legal duties.

O'Connell's attitude to the success of the *Nation* was at best indifferent. He was aware that it was largely responsible for the huge upsurgence in membership into what he saw as *his* movement for Repeal so he didn't dare challenge it. He also noted, with some alarm, that there was a tendency in the *Nation* to discourage the belief that Repeal of the Union could be achieved by purely peaceful means. Though Duffy insisted that nothing explicit was printed there was occasionally the inference.

The young men who ran the paper became an important and popular section of the Repeal Movement and O'Connell came to view them with mistrust. On the other hand, they still acknowledged O'Connell as leader of Repeal and sought no limelight for themselves so he held his disapproval in check. However, there was a growing disillusionment among certain contributors to the *Nation* with O'Connell's autocratic style of leadership and, more significantly, his rigid adherence to the principle of 'moral force only'. (The term 'moral force' in its Irish context, was coined by Thomas Davis and first appeared in print in the *Nation*.) There was also a feeling within the group that O'Connell had allowed Repeal to become identified with exclusively Catholic interests. As supporters of a nationalism which embraced all faiths this was unacceptable to them.

A more confident and vociferous *Nation* faction now began to present itself at Repeal meetings and this unnerved O'Connell. He wasn't used to dealing with people with independent minds who didn't pander to his every whim and certainly weren't in awe of him. Partly to distinguish them from his older and more loyal followers, and partly because of their resemblance to a nationalist movement in Italy called 'Young Italy', he nicknamed them, patronisingly, 'Young Ireland'. It was a name appropriate to their youthful exuberance and nationalist ideals. Inadvertently this nickname would stick and the Young Irelanders were to become a key influence in shaping Ireland's history. They would soon become something of a thorn in O'Connell's side.

## Chapter 4

# Mitchel and the Great Famine

> Then the poor people – God comfort them! They have another famine-winter before them, for the potatoes have generally failed again; and, to be sure, the corn is not for the likes of them.
> 
> —Mitchel's *'Jail Journal'*. October, 1848.

IN SEPTEMBER 1845 YOUNG Ireland and the *Nation* was dealt a devastating blow with the sudden death of Thomas Davis from scarlet fever. Although only thirty years old at the time of his death, Davis was a hugely inspirational figure within Young Ireland and his untimely death deprived it of perhaps its most charismatic personality. His gentle and retiring manner and his sensitivity drew people to him and even his opponents admired him. In every sense, Davis epitomised the spirit, courage and idealism of Young Ireland and he would be irreplaceable among its ranks.

As a writer and poet the Davis legacy is very much with us 160 years later. Still popular today, songs like 'A Nation Once Again' and 'The West's Awake' were penned by him and first appeared in the *Nation* while he was editor. The influence of Thomas Davis on Irish Nationalism persisted long after his death. Davis had completely dedicated the last three years of his young life to the *Nation* and his name would be for ever synonymous with it. His judicious maxim, first expressed in the *Nation*, *'educate that you might be free'*, would be adopted by future generations of Irish Nationalists. John Mitchel, who had been drawn towards the Repeal Movement by Davis, would succeed him as editor and leader writer of the *Nation*.

Thomas Osborne Davis

The *Nation* prophetically wrote in its report on the funeral of Thomas Davis, 'Souls like his never die but make a part of the history and heart of their country forever.' Padraig Pearse wrote of the need, espoused by Davis, for all men and women to unite if Ireland's best interest was to be served. He reminds us in 'The Spiritual Nation' (February1916) that Davis recognised that all Irishmen and women 'are heirs of a common past, a past of spiritual, emotional, and intellectual experience which knits them together indissolubly'.

Many years after Davis's death, Gavan Duffy described him in his book *Young Ireland* (1884) as 'simply the best man I have ever known ... and the most notable Irishman of the generation to which he belonged ... When Davis died it seemed as if the sun had gone out of the heavens.'

The influence of Thomas Davis on later nationalists cannot be overstated and Arthur Griffith, founding member of Sinn Fein in 1905, described him as 'the prophet I followed throughout my life and the man whose words and teaching I tried to translate into practice in politics.' Mitchel wrote of his death as 'a national calamity' and described his close friend Davis as 'a man of imperial genius with a gallant and gentle nature'. He was much loved and greatly missed by all in Young Ireland. In 1854 Mitchel published an edition of the poems of Thomas Davis with an introductory memoir of his friend and early mentor.

Just before Christmas 1845, Mitchel and his family left their secure life in Banbridge and moved to Dublin. The Mitchels had four children at this time and it meant a huge upheaval and an entirely new way of life. Jenny at first was reluctant to uproot but, as in most things, felt it difficult to go against her husband's wishes. Their move to No. 1, Upper Leeson Street, Dublin would coincide with the gravest crisis this country would ever face – An Gorta Mor, The Great Famine.

It was estimated that somewhere between one third and a half of the population of Ireland was completely dependent for their existence on the humble but nutritious potato at that time. It was the staple diet of the tenant farmer the entire year round as it was easy to grow and harvest. Dependency on the potato had been deep rooted for generations so when blight struck the harvest in 1845 the people were completely unprepared. The landlords showed little sympathy for their struggling tenants and the government simply didn't react.

The failure of the potato harvest in autumn 1845 would signal a watershed in modern Irish history and actuate the death of over one million people from starvation and related diseases. It was perhaps the dividing line when centuries of mistrust and opposition would develop into enduring and bitter hatred of England. It would be a hatred that would encompass the globe with the mass emigration which co-existed and followed the Famine. More than any other event, An Gorta Mor would shape the attitude of the Irish race towards England for generations. The Famine, was unquestionably, the highest emotionally charged chapter in Irish history.

The British government when faced with an emergency of such proportion seemed unmoved, even detached, in dealing with it. The magnitude of the disaster cannot be overstated but this should not serve as an excuse for Britain's ineffective and tardy reaction. There was a definite failure by Britain to accept responsibility once the first harvest failed. Widespread starvation existed despite the fact that tenants were growing other crops which were going to the landlords in lieu of rent and being exported to Britain. The resources were there to combat famine, regrettably the resolve was not. For Mitchel the immediate solution was obvious.

In one of his earlier editorials in the *Nation* he warned the landlords against forcing the people to surrender the only food left to them. He followed up his warning with a reminder that hunger and destitution had often aided revolution. His editorship was already showing distinct signs of change from the more temperate style of his predecessor, Thomas Davis. (It would shortly make Gavan Duffy more than a trifle uncomfortable.) Times too were changing drastically from the headier days when Repeal was the main concern of the people.

Mitchel's writing was becoming more anti-English as each edition of the *Nation* appeared. He now wrote of the Famine in unmistakable terms. It was virtual genocide, inflicted on a destitute people by a calculating British government. Its refusal to admit that there was a national calamity in Ireland exonerated their apparent disinterest in seriously tackling it. The government even went so far as to rubbish newspaper reports from Ireland as grossly exaggerated. Much of the English press when it did direct its attention to the Famine, it was usually to minimise it or apportion blame on the 'laziness' of the Irish people. It also on occasions, made reference to the 'ingratitude' of the Irish. There was widespread belief in England, promulgated by the press, that a massive Famine relief programme existed in Ireland, paid for by English taxpayers.

A typical lead story appeared in the *Times* in August 1847, when the crisis was at its worst. Rather than accept that the English government had a moral and political obligation to alleviate the suffering of the Irish people, the *Times* preferred to exploit their plight by pouring scorn on Irish Nationalism. In a despicable attempt to divert attention from the real issue, the *Times* chose to see it as an opportunity to malign outspoken Nationalists like Mitchel and Duffy.

With predictable arrogance the *Times* reported, 'In no other country have men talked treason until they are hoarse, and then gone about begging sympathy from their oppressors. In no other country have the people been so liberally and unthriftily helped by the nation they denounced and defied.' Was Mitchel exaggerating when he wrote in his *Jail Journal* introduction that, 'England may tell what tale she will and all mankind will believe her.'?

New legislation introduced in Westminster could have prevented any major loss of life from starvation or the dreaded typhus fever which accompanied it. The food produced on Irish soil was more than sufficient to sustain her starving population. Mitchel wrote of the food exported to England and grown on Irish soil – 'good and ample provision for double her own population'. His solution was as valid and convincing as ever – keep the food grown on Irish soil in Ireland and keep alive the Irish people. This was followed with the threat – if all else fails, forcefully close the ports to export.

He consistently argued that the Famine was not a natural catastrophe – a visitation by God on an ill-fated people – but an appalling crime perpetrated by a powerful and merciless government. Famine in Ireland was not a 'dispensation of Providence' when the English were feeding well, upon food produced on fertile Irish soil. He later wrote in his *Jail Journal* introduction:

> Without a famine in Ireland, England could not live as she had a right to expect; and the exact complement of a comfortable family dinner in England is a coroner's inquest in Ireland: verdict, Starvation.

There was no place for fudging in Mitchel's analysis and this statement must possibly rank as the most damning indictments ever written of England's indifference to famine in Ireland.

Through his columns in the *Nation*, Mitchel kept up his relentless attack on government policy, or more precisely, the lack of any. As issue followed issue, his language grew ever more damning. Ireland was under British rule, 'the most powerful and prosperous state on earth', so how could such a catastrophe continue unabated without Britain's compliance? As far as Mitchel was concerned, Britain, with all its power and wealth, stood indicted before the world, and he saw it as his mission in life to expose her hypocrisy. As the grip of Famine intensified his hatred of Britain deepened and his rhetoric grew increasingly confrontational.

Britain, he repeatedly emphasised, had taken advantage of the potato blight to starve the Irish people into submission and also saw it as its opportunity 'to thin out the multitudinous Celts'. The census in 1841 showed that the population of Ireland was over eight and a quarter million people and increasing. When the census was repeated in 1851, it revealed the population had fallen to below six and a half million. Mass emigration continued for at least another five years and the population continued to decline. Analysts believe the decrease in population from 1845 to 1851 was well in excess of two million people.

The general belief is that about one million died from starvation and disease and as many as one and a quarter million emigrated to the United States, Canada, Australia and Britain. British ports like Liverpool, Bristol and Glasgow were inundated with fever-ridden and near destitute Irish emigrants. Mitchel describes the scene of a desperate and diseased people flocking to the ports in an effort to be anywhere but Ireland.

> Those who could still scrape up the means fled to the sea, as if pursued by wild beasts, and betook themselves to America.
> —*Last Conquest of Ireland (Perhaps)*

The 'coffin ships' as they came to be known because of the high mortality rate on the long voyage, left Ireland alongside corn-laden vessels bound for British ports. The voyage to America could take up to three months and tens of thousands didn't survive the crossing. It is believed that as many as twenty thousand people died en route to Canada alone. With severe overcrowding and extremely poor sanitation, dysentery was the major killer.

For those who could scrape together the passage, it was foreign shores. For those who couldn't it was the workhouse or the pauper's grave. There was an understandable reluctance among those evicted from their homes to go into the workhouses which had sprung up all over the country. They were places of extreme discomfort and strict discipline and families were immediately broken up – husbands from wives and children from their parents. Initially, the people who did enter these institutions were often the elderly and infirm but they were at least given two basic meals each day and had a roof over their heads. However by 1847, as famine raged out of control, and more and more people were being evicted from their homes, the workhouses rapidly filled up.

It wasn't unheard of in the early stages of the Famine, for people to deliberately commit a fairly trivial offence in order to be sent to prison. It was obviously preferable to the grim prospect of life in the workhouse. Mitchel in his *Jail Journal* writes of the effects of the workhouse on the human psyche. 'A man went in,' he wrote, 'and a pauper came out.' There is also a short, much-quoted anecdote which sums up perfectly the people's attitude to the workhouse.

> A well-meaning traveller once asked a homeless beggar man why he wouldn't seek refuge in the local workhouse. The destitute beggar replied, 'I'd rather share the fox's hole and lie down to die with the air of heaven above me as all my people did, than be put alive into that poor man's gaol and be looked at once a month by the quality like a show.'

Remarkably, Mitchel's theory that Ireland in the 1840s was the victim of an 'artificial famine', overseen by an unsympathetic British government, was shared by few other journalists or economists of his day. His belief that England saw famine as an opportunity to thin out an excess and ever-increasing population was regarded by most of his contemporaries even within Young Ireland as largely unsubstantiated. That one nation could deliberately allow its closest neighbour starve to death and, at the same time, insist that food produced by that neighbouring country leave its shores, was in Mitchel's view, a heinous and calculated crime. Did Arthur Griffith exaggerate greatly when he wrote of Mitchel:

> 'In a land so lost to reason, the voice of sanity was deemed mad.'?

More recently, Mitchel's theory of a 'British sanctioned famine' is given much greater credence and dramatist George Bernard Shaw endorsed it when he wrote simply, 'When a country is full of food and exporting it, there can be no famine.' And throughout the terrible Famine years Mitchel's call to close all Irish ports went unheeded even by his fellow countrymen – the sole voice of a man crazed by the sight of oppression! His was a lone voice not only crying in the wilderness but about the wilderness, a wilderness from which for Mitchel there seemed no escape.

Dr. Christine Kinealy, Professor of History at the University of Central Lancashire, has written extensively on An Gorta Mor and her publications include *This Great Calamity* (1994). Dr. Kinealey's statistics substantiate irrefutably what John Mitchel preached 'until he was hoarse'. She verifies that almost four thousand vessels carried food from Ireland to British ports in 1847. In that same year, four hundred thousand Irishmen, women and children died of starvation and related diseases.

More than ten years after the 'British Sanctioned Famine' – a term Mitchel frequently used in his writing – the horrors he witnessed were still fresh in his mind. *Writing in Last Conquest*, published in 1859, Mitchel describes what he saw on a journey he made to Galway in the depth of winter 1847 – sights in his own words 'that will never wholly leave the eyes that beheld them'. Sights which he described in his *Jail Journal* Introductory (1854), 'that might have driven a wise man mad'.

> Sometimes I could see in front of the cottages, little children leaning against a fence when the sun shone out – for they could not stand – their limbs fleshless, their bodies half-naked, their faces bloated yet wrinkled, and of a pale greenish hue –

children who would never, it was plain to all, grow up to be men and women. I saw Trevelyan's plan in the vitals of these children; his red tape would draw them to death; in his Government laboratory he had prepared for them the typhus poison.

Charles Trevelyan was the administrator of the government's Famine Relief Policy in Ireland and in Mitchel's view, accountable for implementing a more sinister 'population control policy'. Trevelyan, who was Permanent Secretary to the Treasury, was a leading exponent of 'Providentialism'. He had described the Famine in his book *The Irish Crisis* (1848) as 'a direct stroke of an all-wise and all-merciful Providence'. He added in veiled racist terms that the Famine exposed 'the deep and inveterate root of social evil' which existed in Ireland.

There was no doubt in Mitchel's mind that the potato blight had presented the government with the opportunity to rid itself of a looming, over-population crisis in Ireland and the architect of this depopulating policy was Trevelyan. The whole doctrine of 'Providentialism' – divine intervention for the general good – was not a doctrine that had the least shred of credibility in Mitchel's thinking. On where exactly blame for the Famine should be apportioned, he would later write in *Last conquest* (1861),

> The British account of the matter is firstly a fraud and secondly a blasphemy. Although it was the Almighty who sent the potato blight, it was the English who created the Famine.

Trevelyan and his fellow travellers in Government also believed that by depopulation, the 'primitive Irish' might be, in some bizarre way, fast-forwarded to a 'civilised race'.

The dispossession and utter deprivation Mitchel witnessed, particularly the eviction of whole families for non payment of rent, deeply disturbed him. In the terrible winter of 46-47 it is estimated that tens of thousands were evicted from their homes and in excess of half a million during the course of the famine (1845 –52) Entire villages, like Ballinglass (population approx. 300) in Co. Galway, had been evicted in a single day by police and military in March

1846. The landlord wished to turn their holdings into a vast grazing farm and demolished almost sixty homesteads to do so. 'The very children, flung out by the bailiff, to perish in the winter's sleet', is how Mitchel described the needless ravaging of Ballinglass in the *Nation*. Mitchel had nothing but contempt for landlordism and never missed an opportunity to highlight the unscrupulousness of both local and absentee landlords.

The winter of 46-47 was particularly long and severe, and as the grip of Famine deepened, Mitchel felt that the people deserved stronger and more decisive leadership. This brought him increasingly into conflict with O'Connell and his outright call in the *Nation* for the people to unite and collectively refuse to pay rent was too extreme for O'Connell to sanction. He interpreted it as unjustifiable measure tantamount to incitement. Mitchel, on the other hand, saw it as a measure necessary for self-preservation. He was becoming so frustrated with what he saw as O'Connell's outright rejection of any form of physical resistance that it was only a matter of time before they were at loggerheads within Repeal. Mitchel, it should be pointed out, was certainly not advocating armed insurrection, or anything like it, at this stage.

## The Famine Year 1847

The Famine, more than any other issue, profoundly impacted on Mitchel's thinking and politics and his writing in the *Nation* reflected this. If he was a constitutional nationalist before the advent of Famine, he was bordering on revolutionary when it struck for the third successive year. In the summer of 1847, with the effects of Famine reaching horrendous heights and the uncertainty of yet another potato harvest, Mitchel wrote what was possibly his greatest article.

In a June edition of the *Nation* he describes the stark desolation, which confronted him and his companion on an imagined visit to the west of Ireland. He had visited this serenely beautiful part of Ireland two summers previously – before famine gripped the land. The article was simply entitled 'June in the Famine Year'.

On a warm summer's day, John Mitchel sat down in the office of the *Nation* to write a fairly routine article – a review of Irish Guide Books. Out of the beautiful memories they evoked, his thoughts then turned to the Ireland of the day – a desolate land now ravaged by famine with all its terrible effects. Consequently, 'The Famine Year 1847' filled Mitchel's brain and flowed from his immortal pen. It was journalism of the highest quality described by Arthur Griffith as 'the most beautiful and terrible article that has ever come from the pen of an Irish journalist.'

Out of the pages of 'The Famine Year' Griffith claims that 'the John Mitchel of 1848 has his birth' – the angry revolutionary embarking on what he saw as a one-man crusade against the might and main of a powerful and callous empire. Here is a short, haunting extract from that truly exceptional descriptive article.

> But what (may Heaven be about us this night!) – what reeking breath of hell is this oppressing the air, heavier and more loathsome than the smell of death rising from the fresh carnage of a battlefield. Oh misery!
>
> Had we forgotten that this was the Famine Year? And we are here in the midst of those thousand Golgothas that border our island with a ring of death from Cork Harbour all round to Lough Foyle. There is no need of inquiries here – no need of words; the history of this little society is plain before us.
>
> Yet we go forward, with sick hearts and swimming eyes to examine the Place of Skulls nearer. There is a horrible silence; grass grows before the doors; we fear to look into any door, though they are all open or off the hinges, for we fear to see yellow chapless skeletons grinning there; but our footfalls rouse two lean dogs that run from us with doleful howling, and we know by the felon-gleam in their wolfish eyes how they have lived after their masters died. We walk amidst the houses of the dead and out the other side of the cluster, yet there is not one where we dare to enter.

## Chapter 5

# No Union in Repeal

THE DIVISIONS WITHIN THE Repeal Association would come to a head at the historical meeting held in Conciliation Hall, Dublin on 11th July 1846. O'Connell called the meeting to stamp his authority on the Association and facedown any young pretenders. He may have been concerned at the use of more militant language by Mitchel and a few others in recent times but it was more likely a deliberate ploy to force any dissidents out of the association. O'Connell had never been subjected to criticism before and he was certainly not going to accept it from within his own ranks.

For too long O'Connell had been cosseted by 'yes-men' and members of his own family. His third son John, who had always been antagonistic towards 'Young Ireland', was probably the prime motivator in convening the meeting. At the time he was the MP for Kilkenny and had high political ambitions. Three of Daniel O'Connell's sons and two sons-in-law were elected to the Westminster Parliament in the 1832 General Election, such was the extent of his popularity at that time.

John O'Connell proposed that the Association would never, under any circumstances, use force to attain its ends. The 'Peace Resolution' called upon all members to subscribe to the doctrine that national liberty was not worth the shedding of one single drop of blood, and to 'disclaim and abhor all attempts to improve and augment constitutional liberty by force and violence.' O'Connell, on his father's instruction, announced that anyone, who was not prepared to accept the 'Peace Resolution' unreservedly, could no longer remain a member of the Repeal Association.

In the course of the long, and at times, acrimonious debate which followed, Mitchel refused to condemn other societies which in the past had used physical force. In what was otherwise a moderate speech he concluded by referring directly to the United Irishmen of 1798, of which he stated, his father had been a member. 'They believed,' argued Mitchel, 'that liberty was worth some blood letting. Therefore to abhor its use was to abhor their memory and the memory of my own father.' He could not and would not dishonour their memory or denounce their methods. At the time, Mitchel did not directly advocate the use of physical force but believed it might be necessary 'as a last resort'. With Ireland facing its second year of a failed potato harvest and Britain maintaining its indifferent role, he was having serious reservations about the effectiveness of constitutional agitation.

Thomas Francis Meagher a member of Young Ireland followed. In a memorable speech he hailed the sword as a sacred weapon, winning for him the title 'Meagher of the Sword'. Aged only twenty-three he was the son of a wealthy merchant who was also Mayor of Waterford and an ardent O'Connell supporter. This glorification of the sword, or any other weapon for that matter, would not be tolerated and John O'Connell was immediately on his feet shouting Meagher down. He then threatened to leave the hall if Meagher was allowed to continue. Smith O'Brien interrupted O'Connell to state that he could not remain if the right to free speech was being denied Meagher. He then rose to leave and was followed out of the hall by Blake Dillon, Gavan Duffy, Mitchel, Meagher and all other members of Young Ireland. And with them went the support of Ireland's youth and the spirit of Irish nationalism.

At the time of their secession from Repeal, 'Young Ireland' had no plans for armed insurrection. They had really no alternative strategy and their differences with Repeal and 'Old Ireland' were largely of a personal nature. (The question of the use of physical force hadn't been seriously debated within Young Ireland.) They had lost all respect for O'Connell and now doubted his readiness to lead the people from the front. Some in 'Young Ireland' naively believed that the Protestant landed class could be won over to the cause of Irish Nationalism if it was no longer perceived as an inward-looking, Catholic-dominated movement. It is most unlikely, however, that Mitchel subscribed to the belief that the gentry had any positive role to play.

The Repeal Association was now split as O'Connell anticipated it would be when he laid down his divisive 'Peace Resolution' regarding the use of force. He also recognised that the rift between Young Ireland and himself was, at this stage, too deep to be healed and made no attempt to win them back. Repeal was still numerically very strong and he was still its undisputed leader. But O'Connell was seventy years of age, his health was failing and his once alert mind had become confused and agitated. His son John was now making decisions and he was unpopular even among those loyal to his father. The great association O'Connell had founded and dominated for so many years, had lost its brightest young stars and had failed to win Repeal. Six months later, in February 1847, Daniel O'Connell left Ireland for the last time.

Early in November, Mitchel and his fellow seceders from Repeal called a meeting to establish a new national organization. Doubts were freely expressed as to the wisdom of such a move, for the mass of the people still had faith in O'Connell. Despite the failure to win Repeal under his leadership and the deterioration in his sharp intellect, O'Connell was still revered as a national hero. The meeting however was a success and a second meeting was called for 31st January, 1847. Almost one thousand people turned up for this meeting in the Music Hall on Abbey Street and the Irish Confederation, with Smith O'Brien, Meagher and Mitchel as its leaders, was formed.

William Smith O'Brien was the second son of Sir Edward O'Brien a wealthy landowner and baron from Dromoland in Co. Clare. He was believed to be a direct descendant of King Brian Boru. William, with his aristocratic background, received his early education at Harrow, a leading English public school, and later graduated from Cambridge University. He was elected Conservative MP for Co. Clare in 1828 when only twenty-five years of age and later became MP for Co. Limerick in 1835. His older brother, Sir Lucius, was also a Conservative MP.

Having served over eleven years in Parliament, O'Brien realised the hopelessness of securing any measure of justice for Ireland at Westminster and he abandoned Conservatism and converted to Repeal in 1843. He immediately became O'Connell's loyal second-in-command before things turned sour and he became an outspoken critic and opponent. Smith O'Brien was coming to realise that constitutional methods alone might not be enough if self-government was to be won. In time, he came to be regarded as the leader of the Irish Confederation and assumed the title of Chairman of the Council.

Soon the Confederation became a national organisation and clubs sprang up all around the country. Having opposed O'Connell's Peace Resolution in Conciliation Hall, it was somewhat ambivalent itself on the use of force. It neither made threats of war nor pledged itself to using constitutional means only. Its aspirations were the protection of Ireland's national interests and the achievement of legislative independence for Ireland. To achieve these objects its members were prepared to use all means 'consistent with honour, morality and reason'. It had left all options open and ruled nothing in or out. Nevertheless, it seems highly unlikely, that these young idealists had given any serious thought to the reality of having to use forceful means.

## Chapter 6

# Mitchel on O'Connell

BEFORE THE SPLIT IN Repeal, relations between some members of the Irish Confederation and O'Connell, had previously been strained, were now openly hostile. Mitchel, in particular, believed that O'Connell's brand of politics had long outlived its usefulness and that the time would shortly come for 'physical resistance to replace moral force'. (This wasn't quite what the rest of the Confederation believed.) By this time he was in virtual open revolt against England. He saw abject poverty and misery everywhere he looked and was becoming more exasperated with O'Connell's dithering and was rapidly losing patience.

Mitchel was coming to realise that O'Connell, because of his age and possibly the fear of imprisonment, was not prepared to take any risks and lacked the moral courage to lead a people crushed by famine. It is worth remembering that O'Connell was forty years older than Mitchel and might be expected to be more cautious. Of greater importance, Mitchel no longer trusted O'Connell and felt that he would abandon Repeal for the promise of reform if he thought it expedient. As far as Mitchel was concerned nothing short of Repeal – and merely as a stepping stone – was now an acceptable demand.

Mitchel repeatedly poured scorn on O'Connell believing he was dishonest and motivated by self-interest only. He later wrote in his *Jail Journal* (April 1849) of the leader he once respected and admired but had latterly grown to despise:

> Poor old Dan! – wonderful, mighty, jovial and mean old man! With silver tongue and smile of witchery and heart of melting ruth! – lying tongue! smile of treachery! heart of unfathomable

Daniel O'Connell

fraud! What a royal yet vulgar soul! ... with the base servility of a hound and cold cruelty of a spider!

It is difficult to imagine how, what once was respect, could so easily be replaced by utter contempt. Mitchel's tirade of abuse in this instance can best be described as unwarranted. Interestingly, he has adopted an almost Shakespearean style of ridicule, a writer we're reminded in *Jail Journal*, he greatly admired.

In his book *The Last Conquest of Ireland (Perhaps)* published twelve years after O'Connell's death in 1847, Mitchel launches another blistering attack on O'Connell accusing him of

> using his art and eloquence to emasculate a bold and chivalrous nation

He continues his onslaught:

> his continual denunciation of arms degraded the manhood of his nation to such a point that to raise them to resistance in his own cause was impossible.

He concludes his demolition of O'Connell's reputation with probably his most defamatory criticism. In the same paragraph he alleges:

> O'Connell was therefore, next to the British Government, the worst enemy that Ireland ever had, or rather, the most fatal friend.

The reader must make up his/her own mind on the veracity of this statement. It is reasonable to conclude that few but Mitchel would have dared put it in print, given the lofty position O'Connell's memory was still held at that time. The pen, they say, is often mightier, or in this case more destructive, than the sword, and Mitchel wielded a mightily destructive pen.

Mitchel believed that the gratitude and admiration which his early services had won for O'Connell, he forfeited with his weak leadership when Ireland needed him most and the latter part of his life was something of an anti-climax. He says of O'Connell that he was a character imbued with contradictory qualities:

> so capable at once of the highest virtues and the lowest vices, of the deepest pathos and the broadest humour, of the noblest generosity and the most spiteful malignity.

Mitchel claimed that O'Connell cared little for the Irish peasantry and gloried in his power over them, so long as they:

> did their duty and paid the Repeal subscription and, of course, cheered and paraded at the appropriate times.

His criticism of O'Connell in *Last Conquest* seems strangely inconsistent with what Mitchel wrote of O'Connell in his *History of Ireland*.

> Beyond all doubt, his death was hastened by the misery of seeing his proud hopes dashed to the earth, and his well-beloved people perishing; for there dwelt in that brawny frame tenderness and pity soft as a woman's

Here his language and sentiment are clearly more temperate possibly because he was writing a commissioned history and had to keep his personal opinions in check and write dispassionately.

Writing in the *United Irishman* less than a year after O'Connell's death Mitchel once again goes on the offensive. His readership may have had little sympathy for O'Connell but Mitchel was clearly undeterred by the special position O'Connell still held in the nation's heart. Impervious to any adverse reaction or criticism, Mitchel wrote:

> The great Irish aider and abettor of the English plunderers was one Daniel O'Connell, throughout his life the upholder of middle class rule ... and, on all occasions, the enemy of the Irish working class. He was the principal agency by which trade unions and combinations of workmen were broken down in Ireland, and labour left naked and unarmed to the mercy of capital. He upheld landlordism and held down the working farmer to the utmost of his ability.

The broadside on this occasion is largely of a political nature and one of the more explicit examples of a Young Irelander recognizing the importance of the class struggle. In the mid-nineteenth century, radical thinking of this nature was uncommon in Ireland. Around this time Mitchel was coming increasingly under the influence of James Fintan Lalor and this might explain his reference to trade unionism and labour. There is little doubt that what Mitchel witnessed during the Famine altered his essentially conservative views and this in turn left him more receptive to Lalor's doctrine on 'the land issue' and class struggle.

With the passing of time Mitchel certainly didn't mellow in his opinion of the man he once warmly welcomed to Newry as the 'Liberator' and winner of Catholic Emancipation. No other member of Young Ireland was as outspoken or vituperative in their criticism of O'Connell but none possessed Mitchel's talent for burning invective. There is no doubt that O'Connell, even in death, brought out a ferocity in Mitchel he seemed incapable of concealing.

## The Death of Daniel O'Connell 1847

Daniel O'Connell was seventy years old when the Famine began and the suffering of his people broke his health and his spirit. In February 1847 he left Ireland hoping to have an audience with the Pope but he died in Genoa on 15th May. Before O'Connell departed for Rome he made a last desperate appeal in the House of Commons for Britain 'in God's name!' to show compassion and act immediately if the virtual annihilation of the Irish race was to be avoided.

As O'Connell had wished, his heart was sent to Rome for burial and his body laid to rest in an impressive vault in Glasnevin Cemetery in Dublin. (He had been instrumental in purchasing the first acres of the cemetery back in 1831.) Mitchel tells us in his *History of Ireland* that when Smith O'Brien signified his intentions to attend O'Connell's funeral, John O'Connell 'publicly and sullenly forbade him.' The depth of ill feeling between Old and Young Ireland would plumb new depths with the malevolent John O'Connell assuming leadership of Repeal.

Daniel O'Connell's great achievement of securing Catholic Emancipation in 1829 is perhaps overshadowed by his failure to win Repeal. For Mitchel and Young Ireland, this was certainly the case. Few were as overtly critical of O'Connell as Mitchel, but collectively they agreed that years of his ineffectual efforts at Westminster hadn't advanced the call for Repeal one iota. In O'Connell's defence, he had sampled prison life in 1844 and hadn't warmed to it so he was not going to place himself in that position again by adopting a more aggressive stance as Young Ireland would have wished.

Secondly, he still had over thirty MPs at Westminster and still believed that, with a Whig government in power, satisfactory reform could be won. But Ireland was in the grip of famine and the Young Irelanders, swayed by Mitchel, were in no mood for accepting crumbs in the form of reform from any British government. At the time of O'Connell's death, Mitchel and a growing faction within Young Ireland were emergent republican separatists, something O'Connell certainly never embraced in his political lifetime.

With O'Connell's death and the major split within its ranks the previous summer, the Repeal Association went into rapid decline. O'Connell's son John assumed leadership after his father's death but he didn't have any of his father's commanding stature and was disliked even within Old Ireland. He lacked the charisma, energy and eloquence of his father and the movement soon became all but extinct. The political climate had rapidly changed with the emergence of the Young Ireland as a separate political entity and this, more than anything, contributed to the virtual demise of the Repeal Association as a significant force in Irish politics.

Its failure must also be assessed against the backdrop of the Famine. No agitation for political change could be successfully carried on by a plague-stricken and starving people. It was not political change which was uppermost in people's minds but food. While the potato rotted in the ground, popular support for the Association withered in the fetid air. Repeal had been O'Connell's creation, and with or without him as its guiding light, sadly had little further to offer.

The turning point in O'Connell's political fortunes may have been the cancellation of the 'monster meeting' to be held on Sunday 8th October 1843 at Clontarf. On the shores of Dublin Bay, Clontarf had been the scene of Brian Boru's famous victory in 1014. There were a number of similar meetings held in places of historical interest and their main purpose was to demand Repeal with a massive show of strength. O'Connell honestly believed that Britain would be forced to concede Repeal if an overwhelming number of people were visibly and peacefully demanding it.

A crowd, estimated at around a half of a million people, attended the meeting held at Tara in Co. Meath on 15th August. The British Government, anticipating an even bigger rally at Clontarf, and fearing there might be a show of military strength, banned the meeting and threatened force against all who tried to assemble. There was no evidence whatsoever to justify the ban as O'Connell had publicly stated at the Tara meeting in August that he would never endorse the use of physical force. In his own words:

> No political change is worth the shedding a single drop of human blood.

Prime Minister Peel won the war of nerves and O'Connell backed down calling off the rally the afternoon before it was due to take place despite the fact that tens of thousands were already on their way to Clontarf. In the official notice calling off the meeting and dated 7th October (3pm) O'Connell stressed the reason was that the safety of the people could not be guaranteed and therefore it was the 'prudent and humane' thing to do. A young member of the committee which cancelled the Clontarf rally remarked on leaving the meeting 'Ireland was won at Clontarf and now Ireland is going to be lost at Clontarf.' O'Connell's course of action greatly disappointed the *Nation* faction within Repeal and this, in time, would grow to outright mistrust in their leader. It was always going to be a fragile alliance between impetuous 'Young' and cautious 'Old'.

O'Connell, Gavan Duffy and seven others were arrested and charged with conspiracy to overthrow the government. They were tried in February 1844 by a prejudiced judge and jury and O'Connell was sentenced to a year's imprisonment and fined £2000. He appealed the sentence to the House of Lords and, so obviously unfair had his trial been, that the verdict was overturned. He was freed in September after only a few months and he left prison as a hero in the fight for freedom of speech. On his release O'Connell continued to work for Repeal but without any clear strategy. The tactics which had secured Emancipation would not win Repeal and he now knew it. For O'Connell the alternative was too drastic to even contemplate. Dissention among the ranks of the Repeal Association was now inevitable.

Mitchel later described O'Connell's 'climb down' over the Clontarf meeting in his *History of Ireland* as 'O'Connell's greatest treachery'. He also asserted that a massacre at Clontarf might have saved Ireland the slaughter by famine two years later but he failed to explain how. Perhaps he believed that a blood sacrifice of huge proportion was the catalyst Ireland needed for full scale revolution. At the time of the Clontarf meeting Mitchel had just become a member of the Repeal Association, was living in Banbridge and wasn't an established figure within Young Ireland.

## Chapter 7

# Mitchel Leaves the *Nation* and the Confederation

AS THE EFFECTS OF famine deepened, Mitchel's writing in the *Nation* became more militant especially with regard to the seizure of farm produce by the army for export to England. Irish soil was producing each harvest, sufficient provision for double the population of the island. Throughout the Famine, ships had sailed from Irish ports laden with livestock and/or grain on a daily basis. Mitchel encouraged the people to oppose this, by force if necessary, and feed themselves and their children. He was passionate on this issue but was still very much, a lone voice.

The mortality rate among children distressed him greatly and he frequently mentioned the suffering of children in his writing:

> and the little ones, with their liquid Gaelic accents that melted into music for us two years ago; they shrunk and withered together until their voices dwindled to a rueful gibbering, and they hardly knew one another's faces; but their horrid eyes scowled on each other with a cannibal glare.
> —'The Famine Year, '47'

In a country facing its third winter of relentless famine, his call for 'physical resistance at strategic points' was surely reasonable and, as far as Mitchel was concerned, it was heartfelt and morally justifiable. It certainly wasn't revolutionary stuff though many at the time interpreted that way.

He was now coming to the conclusion that the 'whole system of British administration in Ireland would have to be met with resistance at every point'. Through the columns of the *Nation* Mitchel was openly exhorting the people to defend their right to live by keeping their harvest 'within the four seas of Ireland'. He realised that this could not be effective if carried out in isolated areas but had to be universal – 'from the River Foyle to the River Lee'. He pointed out in the *Nation* that the might of the British Army would not be enough to act as bailiffs and cattle drivers in every part of Ireland at once if met by a united and resolute people.

In response to an article in the Tory *Morning Herald* which referred to the usefulness of the railway to carry troops to trouble spots in Ireland, Mitchel wrote in the *Nation* that their iron rails and wooden sleepers would provide excellent materials for the manufacture of pikes and other weapons. It wasn't a very practical suggestion – Mitchel wasn't a very practical man – but it didn't go unnoticed by the authorities. Nor did it go unnoticed by Gavan Duffy.

To make any form of resistance effective Mitchel called for widespread, concerted and firm action. He seemed to retain his belief in the spirit of the people to organise, a belief that few in his day shared. But a dispirited people could not be roused and in the words of Arthur Griffith:

> the Ireland he (Mitchel) preached to shrank from the preacher, preferring to sow its fields for foreigners to reap and die of hunger on its hearthstone – but in Peace.

It was his appeal for united resistance which eventually brought him into open conflict with Gavan Duffy who still owned the *Nation*. He was not prepared to publish strategies which might be considered, in any way, a breach of constitutional politics. Mitchel was now overstepping the 'moral force only' ethos of his paper. Rather than expose Gavan Duffy to court action and possible imprisonment, Mitchel resigned as editor and left the *Nation* in December 1847. It must have been a very difficult decision.

The relationship between owner and editor had grown distinctly tense prior to Mitchel's departure and their friendship would also suffer. The man who had launched Mitchel's career in journalism would shortly become the subject of his abuse. P H Pearse was unambiguous when he wrote of the literary elite in the *Nation*. In *The Spiritual Nation* (February 1916) Pearse states, 'It was not Davis but John Mitchel who was Young Ireland's most powerful prose writer.'

Having severed all connections with the *Nation*, the only platform left to Mitchel for publicising his radical views was the Confederation Clubs. Through the clubs he urged the people

> to obstruct and render impossible the transport and shipment of Irish provisions; to refuse to aid in its removal; to destroy the highways, to prevent everyone, by intimidation, from daring to bid for grain or cattle if brought to auction under distress ....in short, to offer a passive resistance universally, but occasionally, when the opportunity served, to try the steel.

There is little doubt that the militant approach advocated by Mitchel was more radical than anything he, or anyone in the Confederation, had articulated before. He had made up his mind exactly where he stood on 'the physical resistance' issue and there to be was no backtracking or vacillating.

The Confederation leadership, however, still retained the slim hope that Repeal could be won by peaceful means but as the Famine continued its relentless course of devastation unhindered, this seemed less and less likely. Nonetheless, many of the Confederation members were uneasy with Mitchel openly promoting any form of physical resistance. Even in desperate times they seemed unable to shake off their ambivalence regarding the opportune use of 'the steel'.

Other Confederation members like James Fintan Lalor were putting forward fresh political ideas. Fintan Lalor was the son of a wealthy Co. Laois farmer and MP for the county. He had been plagued all his life with poor health and, as a result, led a very secluded life until his late thirties. Lalor argued that what really was important was the ownership of the land which he claimed 'belongs to the people of Ireland'. This, he declared, was the obvious lesson to be learned from the Famine. He totally rejected Repeal as an option and was passionate in his belief that, 'forever henceforth, the owners of our soil must be Irish'.

Lalor advocated linking the question of national freedom, for which the people were not prepared to fight for at that time, with the question of land-ownership for which, in his view, they could be roused into battle. He believed implicitly that only the dispossessed tenants could save themselves and there was no role for the landed-class in either struggle. This simple political doctrine had an immediate appeal for Mitchel and, with Lalor, he was now becoming more and more isolated within the Irish Confederation.

Things came to a head when Mitchel appealed directly to the Confederation Clubs throughout Ireland to secure more arms, especially pikes and to organise. Coming on top of his 'when the opportunity served, try the steel' dictum, he was being perceived by some within the movement as something of a loose cannon. Mitchel's apparent endorsement of 'physical force where deemed necessary' was considered by Smith O'Brien to be 'dangerous and immoral and fatal to the interests of the country, as well as being a breach of the fundamental rules of the Confederation'. It was, for O'Brien, almost a declaration of war in a country unprepared for it.

On 4th February 1848 O'Brien called a full meeting of the Confederation Clubs to publicly censure Mitchel. He pointed out that Mitchel's doctrine was liable to throw the people into a war for which they were totally ill-equipped. Mitchel countered that there was no use in having a Confederation unless it was willing, in so critical a situation, to advise the people it claimed to represent to be prepared to use force. He also argued that no carnage could be as horrific as the 'British-sanctioned' Famine.

Finally he warned that if O'Brien's censure motion was adopted the Confederation would become 'merely one of the long series of moral force agitating associations that had plagued Ireland for the last forty years,' and would show the world that

Thomas Devin Reilly

they had 'thrown the people overboard to placate the gentry'. The meeting lasted two days and much to Mitchel's disappointment, his friends Meagher and Dillon along with Duffy, all supported O'Brien who easily carried the meeting. Of the five hundred and five votes cast just under two hundred supported Mitchel's policy. It was a significant minority nonetheless.

Thomas Devin Reilly, Young Irelander and member of the writing staff of the *Nation* was one of Mitchel's few vocal supporters. Reilly, aged only twenty-three and the son of a solicitor from Monaghan Town, argued that had the people been taught the use of arms, they would not have been decimated by the Famine. Mitchel with his friend John Martin, Devin Reilly and a sizeable group of followers walked out of the meeting.

Again, Mitchel seemed to be some way ahead of most of his fellow Confederates in his analysis of the Famine crisis and was marching to a faster drumbeat than they. Although he did not resign from the Confederation itself but from the governing council, Mitchel had unwittingly relinquished his only remaining platform. This was destined to change in only a matter of days.

Cecil Woodham-Smith, English historian and author, wrote of Mitchel in her masterly book on the Famine entitled *The Great Hunger*:

> John Mitchel was the most remarkable and the most formidable of the Young Ireland leaders. His abilities were outstanding and he possessed an extraordinary hatred directed against the British Government, and an equal talent for burning invective. He also had the gift, which the other Young Ireland leaders lacked, of arousing the masses of the people and inspiring them with intense devotion.

Mitchel was certainly, the most hardline and confrontational of the Young Ireland group and more radical in his thinking than any of his contemporaries. He was driven by his hatred of Britain and this, coupled with the suffering he witnessed daily, may, at times, have clouded his judgement. At the time of his departure from the Confederation in February 1848, he was openly defying the British Government. Within the ruling Council of the Irish Confederation Mitchel was the sole advocate of armed revolution, something, the other members believed the country was completely unprepared for. It wasn't Mitchel's sincerity they doubted but his overall judgement.

## Chapter 8

# The *United Irishman*

EXACTLY A WEEK AFTER Mitchel resigned from the Confederation, on 12th February 1848, a new nationalist weekly made its first appearance. It was called the *United Irishman* and its proprietor and editor was John Mitchel. It had its office on Trinity Street, ominously close to Dublin Castle. Fintan Lalor, Devin Reilly, the poet James Clarence Mangan, and Father John Kenyon all contributed articles to this new publication. Fr. Kenyon was parish priest of Templederry, Co. Tipperary and was a close friend of the Mitchel family. Mitchel's younger brother William was in charge of the technical side of the business and the distribution of the paper.

The paper was priced at 5d and was all the *Nation* had been but bore Mitchel's hallmark from its inception. He had now a free hand to write what he wished and, he did with feverish intensity. In the first edition he confidently asserted that the public was waiting 'to hear some voice, bolder, more intelligible, and more independent of parties and cliques.' The *United Irishman* was that voice and it would speak 'open, honest and outspoken resistance to oppression and would tell the naked truth.' There would be nothing ambivalent or apologetic about the *United Irishman*.

Also in this first issue Mitchel addressed Lord Clarendon directly. He pointed out how their resistance (Young Ireland's) differed from the United Irishmen of 1798 and how they learned from the mistakes made by the 'honourable men of '98'. He finished by openly challenging the Lord Lieutenant to place a government spy in the very office of his paper. They had nothing to hide. It certainly was a bold editorial and Mitchel set out his stall from day one.

> We differ, not one iota in principle, but in the mode of action. Theirs was a secret conspiracy, ours is a public one. They had not learned the charm of open, honest resistance to oppression; and through their secret organisation you wrought their ruin. We defy you, and all the informers and detectives that British corruption ever bred. No espionage can tell you more than we will proclaim once a week upon the house-tops. If you desire to have a Castle detective employed about the United Irishman office in Trinity Street, I shall make no objection provided the man be sober and honest.

The paper advocated total separation from England as espoused by 'the illustrious conspirators of '98' and Mitchel now freely asserted the right of the people to use arms if this was the only course left to them. In one of the last editions to appear before the paper was suppressed, he wrote, 'Let the man among you who has no gun sell his garment and buy one.' It was stirring stuff, no doubt, but was also grist to the mill for the staff in Dublin castle.

Time and again Mitchel returned to the pressing issue of the food produced on Irish soil – enough food to 'sustain in life and comfort all the inhabitants of the island'. Mitchel wrote of this abundance of food:

> That wealth must not leave it (Ireland) another year – not until every grain of it is fought for in every stage, from the tying of the sheaf to the loading of the ship.

This call in the *United Irishman* (29th April) would be submitted in evidence at Mitchel's trial less than a month later.

The *Nation* and the *United Irishman* were not seen as rival papers as they shared a common ideology. Both papers were strongly patriotic and appealed to a similar readership. However, the *United Irishman* used much more militant and emotive language. Mitchel and his young co-writer, Devin Reilly, were honest and direct in their appeal to the people to organise, arm and drill. Mitchel advised:

> instead of Parliamentary and constitutional agitation, voting and legal shouting that there be a deliberate study of the theory and practice of guerilla warfare in Ireland.

It was rousing rhetoric of a type not evident before and was generating a great deal of attention, not all of it favourable. In Mitchel's Introductory to *Jail Journal* he wrote that the *'United Irishman* was established specifically as an organ of Revolution.'

Mitchel rarely wrote with such intensity and fierce conviction as he did during the short lifespan of the *United Irishman*. Through its columns he defiantly invited Lord Clarendon, the Queen's Viceroy in Ireland, to prosecute him. He repeatedly reminded the Viceroy that the only way he could silence him was by 'packing a jury'. There was no other the way they would secure a conviction against him in an Irish court. 'Pack away then,' he taunted,

> I expect no justice, no courtesy, no indulgence from you; and if you get me within your power I entreat you to show me no mercy as I, so help me God, would show none to you.

It was blatantly provocative, and Mitchel's articles were eagerly awaited each week. His confrontational style was rousing the people to a level of enthusiasm not witnessed for some time. It was also evident to most that Mitchel was right when he boasted that 'Ireland was too small to hold both him and the British Government much longer – one would have to go'. He was on a one-man crusade against an empire and there could be only one outcome. Mitchel was effectively writing his way into exile but seemed undaunted.

Lord Stanley in the British House of Lords warned the government of the strength of character of the men who published the *United Irishman*:

> These men are honest; they are not the kind of men who make their patriotism the means of barter for place or pension. They are not to be bought off by the Government of the day for a

> colonial place… No; they honestly repudiate this course; they are rebels at heart; and they are rebels avowed who are earnest in what they say and propose to do. My belief is that such men are dangerous.

It was a glowing tribute – well be it unintentional and from an unexpected source – but its accuracy is beyond question.

Mitchel's open defiance of British authority coupled with his fire-spitting rhetoric could only be interpreted as incitement and would not be tolerated for long by Dublin Castle. On the evening of 13th May, Mitchel and Devin Reilly were arrested and charged with publishing seditious material. A few weeks later Fintan Lalor, along with John Martin, founded the *Irish Felon* as a successor to the suppressed *United Irishman*. In July, they also were arrested and charged with the same offence as their former editor. Mitchel of course made the Castle's job easier and it didn't have any real need of a spy in his office to gather evidence.

The case against Mitchel was based largely on a 'treasonable speech' he had made and an open letter he had written to the Protestants of Ulster. In the letter Mitchel wrote:

> Religious hatred has been kept alive in Ireland longer than anywhere in Christendom, just for the simple reason that the Irish landlords and the British statesmen found their own account in it; and as soon as Irish landlordism and British dominion are finally rooted out of the country, it will be heard of no longer in Ireland, any more than it is in France or Belgium now.

Written back in 1848, over a century and a half ago, this statement is still as thought provoking and relevant as ever. It also gives us a clear indication of Mitchel's feelings on religious bigotry and whose interest, he believed, it best served.

Thomas Devin Reilly was released on bail and escaped to New York where he worked as a journalist. He died suddenly in Washington less than six years later at only 29 years of age. He was a young man of great courage, outstanding literary ability, and remained immensely loyal to Mitchel. On hearing of Devin Reilly's death in March 1854, Mitchel wrote:

> The largest heart, the most daring spirit, the loftiest genius of all Irish rebels in these latter days sleeps now in his American grave.

Though they had known each other but a short time the bond between them was very close, so close that Devin Reilly later named his first son, who tragically died in infancy, after John Mitchel. Reilly spent much of his time in the Mitchel home and was looked upon by the Mitchel children as a big brother figure. In one of his last articles in the *United Irishman* Devin Reilly wrote of his spiritual leader Mitchel:

> This one man who now lies in jail, resolved that the people should not be deserted, that they should not be sold or sacrificed to any class, that they should not be wholly pauperised, wholly robbed, wholly starved without a struggle. He staked his life and liberty on that. He knew that if they did not strike out for their own lives it was because no man had dared to show them how. He showed them how… And as he walked into Newgate Prison he triumphed.

In all, sixteen editions of the *United Irishman* were published, the final edition appearing on 27th May 1848. In a short and controversial lifetime it had certainly remained faithful to its original claim 'to be open, honest and outspoken against oppression'. Mitchel had used his paper to highlight British domination in Ireland and hoped that, through its columns, he might rouse the people to rebel against it. Through his writing he also hoped to provoke Lord Clarendon – 'Her Majesty's Executioner General in Ireland' – into arresting him. He mistakenly believed that the people would take this as their cue to rebel. He had pinned his hopes for rebellion on a decimated and dispirited people.

## Chapter 9

# Trial and Transportation

> I do not repent anything I have done and I believe that the
> course which I have opened is only commenced.
> —*Mitchel before sentence on him was pronounced.*

FROM HIS CELL IN Newgate Prison, Mitchel's language and mood was as upbeat as ever when he wrote, 'The music my country men love best to hear is the rattle of arms and the ring of the rifle.' It may not have been altogether true giving the despair of the people but it certainly was what Mitchel wished to hear. His belief that the time for insurrection had arrived remained strong. When visited by a deputation from the Confederate Clubs asking him to sign a prepared statement disapproving any attempt to rescue him, Mitchel flatly refused. Many Confederate members in Dublin were now in favour of insurrection and believed a rescue bid for Mitchel might serve as the catalyst they badly needed.

The deputation however, stressed that the leadership of the Confederation believed the time was not right for armed rebellion and that the people were still totally unprepared. Francis Meagher, recognised as the military expert within the Confederation, was particularly convinced that insurrection at that time would only end in slaughter. Meagher was not part of the prison delegation and his views could only be relayed second hand. Mitchel thanked the delegation for their honesty but held firm to his belief that they were wrong and the time was right. With a promise of definite action in the autumn, after the harvest, Mitchel's visitors bade him a sad farewell.

On 25th May John Mitchel's trial began, in Green Street Court,

Dublin, Baron Lefroy acting as presiding judge. Mitchel had been taken from Newgate Prison by an underground passage and stood impassively in the dock. From the outset, he felt confident of victory. No twelve Irishmen, chosen at random, would unanimously agree he was guilty of any crime and his acquittal would be a blow to the prestige and power of British rule in Ireland. On the other hand, if the verdict were to go against him and he was convicted by a 'packed jury', this would send out a clear message to the rest of the world that justice in Ireland was a 'sham and a mockery'. As far as Mitchel was concerned it was a case of 'they're damned if they do and they're damned if they don't'.

Leading counsel for the defence was a very elderly Robert Holmes. As a Protestant he was eligible for the Queen's Bench but had opted to remain at the 'Outer Bar'. It was nearly half a century since Robert Holmes had last represented a client in the Green Street Courtroom. The prisoner on that occasion had been his brother-in-law, Robert Emmet, and he had watched with tear-filled eyes as Emmet left the dock for the scaffold.

The veteran counsellor began Mitchel's trial by challenging the make-up of the jury but was informed by Baron Lefroy that the 'panel was a good and honest one'. This, despite the fact that the foreman of the jury John Whitty, was a unionist politician and not one of the twelve jury members bore an Irish name. During the trial, which lasted two days, Robert Holmes defended his client bravely but realised that there would be no acquittal verdict for his client in this courtroom. In his summing-up to the court, Holmes made a last appeal to the jury's sense of honour and justice, even appealing to their patriotism but knowing in his heart it was all to no avail.

On Saturday 27th May, John Mitchel stood in the dock for sentencing. Baron Lefroy, Sheriff of Dublin, firstly dwelt on the seriousness of the charge and then spoke of the apprehension with which he and his two fellow-magistrates had deliberated on their decision. He then addressed the prisoner directly:

## A Cause Too Many 67

Under the Treason-Felony Act (1848) the sentence of this court is, that you, John Mitchel, be transported beyond the seas for the term of fourteen years.

The general public received the pronouncement with an audible gasp of disbelief at the severity of the sentence. This was quickly followed by a more audible muttering which filled the courtroom. There were shouted demands for order from court officials. Then Mitchel, experiencing at first hand the British judicial system in action, concentrated all the anger and disdain that had been gathering in his heart for two days. In a brief salvo to the court he castigated the Bench:

Neither the jury, nor the judges nor any man in this court presumes to imagine that it is a criminal who stands in this dock. I have shown what the law is made of in Ireland. Her Majesty's Government sustains itself in Ireland by packed juries, partisan judges and perjured sheriffs...

After an attempted rebuke from Baron Lefroy, Mitchel continued in full flight, defending his actions and issuing a stern warning to the court authorities:

I have acted all through this business, from the first, under a strong sense of duty. I do not repent anything I have done and I believe that the course which I have opened is only commenced.

This declaration was greeted with a wild chorus of support and Mitchel, waving to his friends, was hustled from the courtroom to his cell below.

With the possibility of revolt looming on the streets of Dublin, he was moved within hours to a government steamer the *Shearwater* anchored in the River Liffey. Mitchel's long and eventful voyage to the other side of the globe had begun. He reminds us in *Jail Journal* that when he was taken out from the prison 'dark crowds of people were standing about in perfect silence... and amidst all that multitude, the clanking of my chain was the loudest sound.'

Mitchel was first taken to Spike Island, a notorious convict prison at the entrance to Cork Harbour until his final destination was decided. The court had not informed him but his place of exile for the next fourteen years was to be Van Diemen's Land, an island penal colony off the south coast of Australia. (At the time, the authorities weren't sure where his final place of exile was to be.) Van Diemen's Land is known today as Tasmania.

The Council of the Irish Confederation issued a strongly worded address to the Irish people in response to Mitchel's conviction. In it, the Council stated that Mitchel's only offence was 'a love for Ireland as intense as his hatred of foreign oppression'. The Council went on to explain that 'though they may not have shared all Mitchel's opinions, they do not deny that they were dictated by the purest of motives, were maintained with consummate ability, and vindicated with heroic fortitude'.

Further in their address they accuse the British government of 'framing a special enactment to tear Mitchel from his family and his country'. The accusation continues: 'None will contradict us when we affirm that Mr. Mitchel has been found guilty by a jury elected not to TRY but to CONVICT him'. The address concludes by exhorting the people to unite and prepare for 'the final struggle against usurpation and injustice'.

Mitchel might have expressed this particular sentiment a lot more forcefully but then he was commencing a journey to the other side of the world for that precise reason.

## Chapter 10

# *Jail Journal* (1848 -53)

The personal memoranda of a solitary captive.
—John Mitchel in his Introductory (1854)

WITH WRITING MATERIALS AT hand and long lonely hours in which to write, Mitchel decided to keep a journal or diary, which would later be published in 1854 as his *Jail Journal*. It is popularly regarded today as a classic in prison literature and is described by Cecil Woodham-Smith as 'a minor masterpiece which has won Mitchel immortality'.

Mitchel backdated his first entry to the day he left Dublin Bay on board the *Shearwater*. In his opening entry, dated 27th May, 1848, he gets straight to the point. There is clearly no indication of remorse and again he is contemptuous of the British system of justice in Ireland:

> On this day, about 4 o'clock in the afternoon, I, John Mitchel was kidnapped and carried off from Dublin, in chains, as a convicted 'felon'.
>
> I had been in Newgate Prison for a fortnight. An apparent trial had been enacted before twelve of the castle jurors... and a 'conviction' (as if there were law, order, government or justice in Ireland). Sentence had been pronounced by Lord Lefroy – fourteen years' transportation; and I had returned to my cell and taken leave of my wife and two poor boys.

In the same entry in his *Journal* again dated 27th May, Mitchel writes movingly about his departure from his family at Charlemont Bridge, Dublin. He believed that he might never see some of them again and his parting from Jenny and their five children he found most distressing:

> At Charlemont Bridge in Dublin this evening, there is a desolate house – my mother and sisters, who came up to see me (for the last time in case of the worst) — five little children very dear to me; none of them old enough to understand the cruel blow that has fallen on them this day, and above all — above all — my wife.

John Mitchel's *Jail Journal* chronicles his life during his first five and a half years in exile, the final entry being on 29th November, 1853 when he arrived in America after his daring escape from Tasmania. He concludes his 'Journal' when he is reunited with his mother in Brooklyn, New York on that date.

> Without entering the city at all, we pass straight over to Brooklyn where my mother awaits our arrival; and here ends my Journal.

A large portion of his *Jail Journal* is devoted to Mitchel's two-year voyage aboard different prison ships to Van Diemen's Land. The 'asthma demon' which dogged him most of his life was very bad, and for long periods left him extremely weak through lack of sleep. For a few short months he thought that he had at last shaken off the 'fiendish asthma' and the change in climate had 'finally exorcised him' but there was to be 'no escape from this infernal plague'. 'Almighty God!' he cried out as he tossed restlessly in his narrow bed, 'Is the angel Sleep to visit me never more?'

*Jail Journal* is, for many, what immediately springs to mind when the name John Mitchel is mentioned but the title is somewhat misleading. It is not, what one might expect at first glance – the diary of a man's incarceration with all the associated deprivation and hardship. Yes, he was denied his freedom and was exiled from his native land as a 'convicted felon', but he didn't have to spend any protracted period of time languishing in a dank 19th-century prison. His imprisonment was confined to prison ships – five in all – and on arrival in Van Diemen's Land, few restrictions were placed upon him. It would be grossly unfair however, to trivialise in any way, the severity of the court sentence handed down on Mitchel. He may have been spared much of the hardship and degradation of prison life but banishment from 'the land of his birth' was cataclysmic for Mitchel. The punishment lay in the pain of being exiled.

Little of *Jail Journal* then has to do with imprisonment and all its connotations, but is more a collection of reflections, reviews, observations and debates. It contains Mitchel's thoughts and philosophic ruminations on a variety of subjects ranging from the morality of suicide to the glorification of war, from prison reform to the hypocrisy of modernism. An entry, dated New Year's Day 1850, is worthy of mention. Mitchel shares with the reader his approval of 'the blood sacrifice' – a passage which may help explain Pearse's great admiration for his rhetoric. Mitchel writes,

> The blood of fighting men for freedom is never shed in vain – the earth will not cover it up – from the ground it cries aloud... If Ireland in '82, (Grattan's Parliament) instead of winning her independence from the coward by the mere flash of the unbloody sword had, like America, waded in carnage to her freedom, like America she had been free this day.

The style and content are very similar to what Pearse was articulating some sixty years later.

In *Jail Journal* Mitchel shares his views on the wide range of books he read on board the various ships, books often given to him by the ships' doctors and officers. He was insatiable when it came to reading material and read anything from obscure autobiographies and 'indigestible' travel books, to Homer and Shakespeare. Much of it he typically describes as 'vast oceans of tripe!' but concedes that at least it helped pass the interminably lonely nights.

Sir Walter Scott's *Ivanhoe* (devoured for about the fifth time!) and *The Heart of Midlothian* are novels he does write favourably about. Walter Scott's fellow countryman, the writer Thomas Carlyle also comes in for high praise. Mitchel, never a man to lavish praise lightly, writes of Carlyle as 'The only man in these latter days who produces what can properly be termed books.' (26th October '49)

As might be expected, *Jail Journal* contains several references to the prevailing Irish political scene and we are entertained to the writer's judgment on the associated players. On a number of occasions Gavan Duffy comes in for severe personal criticism – 'an unfortunate man evidently cowed and prostrated to the earth'. Daniel O' Connell, as detailed in Chapter 6, is far from immune to Mitchel's critical analysis. That much-quoted and contemptuous portrait of O'Connell where he is described as:

> that royal yet vulgar soul! With the keen eye and potent swoop of a generous eagle of Carn Tual – with the base servility of a hound and the cold cruelty of a spider!

is from an entry dated 22nd April 1849. He does conclude his 'assassination' in a more charitable note with a prayer that 'the Irish earth may lie light on O'Connell's breast... and may God have mercy upon his soul.' His comments on other key players like Smith O'Brien and Francis Meagher are much more sympathetic.

Occasionally Mitchel received newspapers along with the mail or had ones smuggled to him by his guards – 'contraband intelligence' as he referred to it. The English newspapers – 'my sole channel of intelligence' – and letters from home kept him fairly well informed about events, or lack of them, in Ireland. While there was general revolutionary movement throughout Europe, Mitchel observed that,

> Poor, sick, Celtic Ireland, in the meantime is miserably quiet, nobody daring to utter one honest word about public affairs for fear of the Castle-vigour. (15th January 1849)

There are also many excellent examples of Mitchel's talent for free-flowing, vibrant prose to be enjoyed. Often in that fertile imagination he returns to Ireland and reflects on the seasonal changes and associated beauty in that fair land separated by six thousand miles of sea. In an entry dated September 1849, he writes of hearing some Irish air, sung at dead of night, by an Irish prisoner on board the *Neptune*. It immediately carries him back to 'old days when I heard the same air to the humming accompaniment of the spinning wheel'. The nostalgia then gives way to rage and the exile Mitchel curses his captors,

> How fervently I curse the British Empire that Empire of Hell!
> When will thy cup of abomination be full?

Mitchel spent nine dreary months on board the hulk *Dromedary* anchored off Bermuda and tells us he once briefly contemplated suicide so 'solitary and monotonous was his existence'. He decided against, believing that it would be interpreted as an admission that he was a 'felon' and couldn't face up to the reality of it. In an entry dated 14th July 1848, he wrote:

> I may be nicknamed a felon by their Parliament, but if I, in despair, rush to my death, I will own myself a felon, and send my children scandalised to their graves, as the children of a self-convicted criminal and despairing suicide.

Although legally classified as a convicted felon, Mitchel didn't have to do any convict labour like the other prisoners on board and didn't associate with them in any way. He was allowed to wear his own clothes, had access to books and newspapers, and was assured by his superintendent that 'nobody here has any disposition to add to the annoyance he was forced to suffer'. Initially his accommodation was extremely cramped – something of 'a dog house' infested with cockroaches and measuring six feet square – but he was later given his own small cabin with porthole and two shelves of books and for a time had a servant who cooked and cleaned for him. He was also permitted to walk on deck when he pleased so long as the other prisoners were at work or in their quarters.

Parliament had debated his transportation and had decided that 'Mr. Mitchel was to be treated as a person of education and a gentleman.' The same Parliament had passed the Treason-Felony Act only weeks before which classified Mitchel as a felon, now decided he was not to be treated as a common criminal. A gentleman apparently can be a felon but, because of status, should not be treated as one. It all may appear somewhat discriminatory, but Mitchel apparently had no objections and, as he rightly pointed out at his trial, 'neither judge, jury nor any man perceived him as a criminal'. He infers in *Jail Journal* that the preferential treatment he received was due to representation from leading Irish figures in New York to the British government.

On 22nd April 1849, Mitchel left Bermuda on board the convict ship the *Neptune* bound for the Cape of Good Hope in South Africa. On the *Neptune* he had his own cabin and was one of three hundred convicts aboard. For three months the *Neptune* floundered about in the Atlantic and when land was at last sighted it was not South Africa but South America. On 12th August the *Neptune* began her second attempt to reach the Cape and on 19th September sailed into Simon's Bay, twenty miles from Cape Town. The inhabitants of the Cape refused to allow their colony to be turned into a penal settlement and the *Neptune*, with its entire crew and passengers, lay in Simon's Bay for five weary months. Mitchel's asthma returned and for two months he was as seriously ill as he had been in Bermuda.

On the 13th February 1850, word arrived that the *Neptune* was to proceed forthwith to Van Diemen's Land. The colonists had won their fight not to have their land turned into a penal colony by their British masters. As compensation for their hardship and detention, all prisoners on arrival in Tasmania would receive from 'Her Gracious Majesty', a conditional discharge. There was to be one notable exception – prisoner 2014, John Mitchel. His case, according to the government authority Lord Grey, 'being entirely different from all the others and is reserved for separate consideration.'

The six week voyage to Tasmania was for Mitchel a nightmare. His health failed again and only sheer force of will kept him alive. On the morning of 7th April the tiny *Neptune* dropped anchor at Hobart, the main port of Tasmania. The final stage of those 'seafaring horrors' was over. Mitchel had spent almost a year on board the *Neptune* – 'this ship of evil omens, rigged with curses, freighted with hell' – and how he longed to set foot on some shore, any shore 'where there shall be no more sea'.

Hobart must have been, if not a welcoming sight, a source of considerable relief for Mitchel. However, his description in *Jail Journal* dated 7th April 1850, gives us an interesting insight into his opinion of it and, more significantly, of the common lawbreaker:

> Hobart Town, that metropolis of murders and university of burglary and all subterhuman abominations... Hobart Town, Hobartia: Coat of arms – a fleece and a kangaroo with its pocket picked.

Those 'seafaring horrors' hadn't affected Mitchel's acerbic sense of humour!

During his two year ordeal, from leaving Ireland to his arrival in Tasmania, Mitchel was, in most instances, treated with due respect and courtesy. In spite of the official restrictions made on him as a prisoner, his jailers made life on board ship as tolerable as possible. He certainly was not treated as a common criminal and had privileges bestowed on him beyond what he might have expected. But he was still a prisoner of Her Majesty's Government and deeply resented all its implications. To the end of his days Mitchel was at pains to point out that 'no man who loved Ireland ever proclaimed himself to be a criminal'. Criminalisation was as deplorable to Mitchel as it would be to later generations of Irish political prisoners.

Arthur Griffith in his preface to M.H. Gill's edition of *Jail Journal* wrote,

> Here a great character pours itself out, exalting the spirit in the best of us, banishing from us the thought of pity for the prisoner, and replacing it by exultation of him whose free soul no prison may confine, no fate can daunt. It is a book none who has read it once will not read again and again, and say of its author – This is a Man.

## CHAPTER 11

# Young Ireland Rebellion 1848

> Their decision was wrong (not to begin the insurrection in Dublin streets and on the day of my removal) and, as I firmly believe, fatal. But that their motives were pure, and their courage unquestionable, I am bound to admit.
>
> —*Jail Journal* Introductory

THE ARREST OF MITCHEL convinced many in Young Ireland that the only hope now lay in rebellion. Inspired by events in France earlier that year they began hurriedly and recklessly to organise. The English authorities, through its spies in the Irish Confederation, were fully aware that insurrection was being planned for after the harvest when the people would at least have food. They decided it would be wise to strike first. The *Nation* was banned and many of the leaders of Young Ireland including Gavan Duffy were arrested and held without trial.

William Smith O'Brien, Thomas Francis Meagher, John Blake Dillon and other Confederation leaders were in the south when these events happened. They were ill-equipped for military action but nevertheless travelled across Kilkenny and Tipperary trying to get the country people to join them in a rising. They set up their headquarters in Kilkenny where they hoped later to proclaim a Provisional Government and issue instructions to the people.

As they made their way round the countryside, large crowds of people gathered to hear them. Ragged and hungry, they hoped firstly to be fed and then issued with arms but the rebels had neither to offer. There was talk of looting local houses of the gentry for provisions and any weaponry stored there but Smith

O'Brien, as leader, would not countenance such activity. This, he believed, would merely defile their cause and he often ordered the people to go home. Arthur Griffith later described Smith O'Brien as 'noble and fearless but the most unfitted man in Ireland to lead an insurrection.' Mitchel, in *Jail Journal*, wrote something along similar vein.

After almost a week of indecision the insurgents eventually made their way to Ballingarry in Co. Tipperary. A company of approximately fifty police officers was dispatched there and immediately took over a house belonging to the Widow McCormack. Unfortunately for O'Brien and his followers who greatly outnumbered the RIC, there were five McCormack children still inside the house though their mother was outside remonstrating with the crowd. A group of miners proposed blowing up the house with explosives if the children's release could be negotiated. A less extreme measure suggested was to smoke them out using a trailer of smouldering hay. O'Brien was now on the horns of a dilemma. The police refused to release the children and he couldn't in conscience, jeopardise their safety, so a standoff took place.

William Smith O'Brien

While O'Brien was trying to negotiate with the RIC, someone threw a large stone through the kitchen window and the police immediately opened fire. Two of the insurgents were killed and a number wounded in the short skirmish which followed. Smith O'Brien, fearing further bloodshed, ordered his followers to disperse. This simply illustrated just how poorly equipped and unprepared the rebels were. The Young Ireland Rebellion of 1848 was crushed before it seriously began, on a warm summer's day in late July. The *Times* newspaper derogatorily described the attempted rising as 'The Cabbage Garden Revolution' but the outcome might have been different had the McCormack children not been held hostage.

John Blake Dillon, who was present at Ballingarry and was speaking from personal knowledge of the situation, estimated the armament of the insurgents at 'about thirty rust-eaten, fowling pieces, with an average of one round of ammunition for each'. With a greater number of pikes, pitchforks and miners' tools, it was still hardly the appropriate weaponry to face the resources of an empire.

Mitchel later described the insurrection in his *Jail Journal* as

> a poor extemporised abortion of a rising in Tipperary headed by Smith O'Brien

He also wrote in the same entry (24th October 1848) that the insurrection

> has been too long deferred and no rising must begin in the country; Dublin streets for that.

He still held firm to the belief he first expressed to the Confederation delegation which visited him in Newgate Prison shortly before his trial. The correct time to strike was immediately after his arrest and, given the present condition of the island, he argued, the streets of Dublin was the only place for a rising.

He continued his criticism in *Jail Journal* of the whole botched affair, referring in particular to the long-term effect of such ignominious defeat:

What glee in Dublin Castle and in the bloodthirsty dens of Downing Street at this excuse for 'vigour'! And, of course, all the world thinks Irish resistance is effectually crushed; and that Ireland's capacity for resistance was tested at this cursed Ballingarry.

Mitchel, who had favoured revolution only two months before Ballingarry, was now utterly contemptuous of its failure.

O'Brien and Meagher along with Terence Bellew McManus from Liverpool and Pat O'Donoghue were arrested and tried in Clonmel for high treason. They were sentenced to death but this was later commuted to penal servitude for life. They would shortly join John Mitchel as exiles in Van Diemen's Land.

Some of the leaders including Blake Dillon, James Stephens and John O'Mahony escaped to France and America. Stephens, from Co. Kilkenny, had been wounded at Ballingarry and to save him from capture his family pretended he was dead. They even sent obituary notices to the local Kilkenny papers and staged a mock funeral, burying a coffin full of stones. Meanwhile, having been nursed back to health, Stephens slipped away and, after many adventures, he eventually reached Paris.

More than three years after the Munster Rising, Mitchel met up with Smith O'Brien in a hotel in Avoca, Tasmania. The two men hadn't met since Mitchel's trial and, according to Mitchel, he had difficulty recognizing his former associate who had 'lost much of his erect form and stately step. Yet he is a rare and noble sight to see: a man who cannot be crushed, bowed or broken.' The pair later walked up the Glen of South Esk and O'Brien gave his detailed account of the Young Ireland Rebellion. He attributed their failure, in great part, to the behaviour of the priests or what Mitchel preferred to call it 'the priestliness of the priests'.

It should be pointed out that these are not O'Brien's exact words but Mitchel's recording in *Jail Journal* (15th October 1851) of the gist of his conversation with O'Brien. It has clearly been given Mitchel's distinctive 'make-over' with his inimitable capacity for sarcasm. There is also a degree of irreverence.

> Priests hovered around him everywhere; and, on two or three occasions, when the people seemed to be gathering in force, they came whispering round, and melted off the crowd like a silent thaw... but there was his reverence, and he said that if they shed blood they would lose their immortal souls... So they slunk home to take care of their paltry souls and wait for the sheriff's bailiff to hunt them into the poorhouse.

Despite the failure of their insurrection, the Young Irelanders were to become role models and left a rich legacy for future generations of Irish Nationalists. They brought patriotism, honesty and national pride into the public life of Ireland and elevated literature to an unprecedented level. They captured the national imagination with their unsullied vision of an Ireland free to pursue its own destiny. Davis and Duffy had shown the need to unite Catholic and Protestant; Lalor had highlighted the importance of linking land ownership with Nationalism; and Mitchel, Meagher and Reilly had revived Tone and Emmet's dream of an Irish Republic. They were, of course, a curious mix and, it's fair to say, were not all committed separatists.

The tragic lesson to be learned from the failure of their Rebellion was that, without careful and vigilant planning, only inglorious defeat can follow. Most of the Young Irelanders were simply not revolutionaries, nor did they really understand what revolution demanded. Their knowledge of military tactics was, at best, basic. They were, with the odd exception, a group of well intentioned, romantic figures with an immense love for Ireland and in return were much loved. It's a measure of their standing that, despite 'cursed Ballingarry', they still hold a unique place in Irish history and hearts today.

## Chapter 12

# Van Diemen's Land

THE AUTHORITIES IN HOBART Town assigned Mitchel and John Martin to Bothwell, a village forty six miles from Hobart. In *Jail Journal* dated 13th April 1850, Mitchel describes the remote village:

> The village of Bothwell, where John Martin and myself are now privileged, by 'ticket of leave' to live or to vegetate, contains about sixty or seventy houses; has a church where clergymen of the Church of England and of Scotland perform service, one in the morning and the other in the evening of Sunday; has four public houses or hotels, establishments which are much better supported and have much larger congregations than the church.

John Martin had been sentenced to ten years 'transportation beyond the seas' and he was a great support for Mitchel while in exile. No one was closer to Mitchel than John Martin and Mitchel described his friend as 'retiring, quiet, and contented by temperament and habit, one who lived always for others, never for himself.' Martin had qualified as a doctor but decided he didn't wish to practice medicine preferring instead the life of a gentleman farmer though 'of small means'.

In *Jail Journal* Mitchel often refers to his good friend by the nickname John Knox. This curious name was bestowed on Martin by Kevin Izod O'Doherty, a young Dublin medical student, who had been transported for ten years in 1849. Like Mitchel, he had been indicted on a treason-felony charge for publishing seditious material in the *Irish Tribune*. O'Doherty, in turn, is frequently referred to in *Jail Journal* as Saint Kevin.

John Martin

Mitchel either didn't have a nickname or was not prepared to reveal it to his readers.

Shortly after his arrival on the island Mitchel had accepted his 'ticket of leave'. All the other Young Ireland exiles, with the exception of Smith O'Brien, had also accepted the 'ticket'. This was basically a promise that the bearer would not attempt to escape from the penal colony. In return he was allowed to move freely in the Bothwell district but was not allowed to make contact with any of the other Irish prisoners and had to report to the district police-magistrate once a month.

In June 1851, Jenny and their five children arrived from Ireland. In an unusually brief entry, dated 20th June, Mitchel wrote in *Jail Journal*:

> Today I met my family once more. Things cannot be described.
> Tomorrow morning we set off through the woods for Bothwell.

It was more than three years and thousands of miles of ocean since the Mitchels had been a complete family.

In August, the Mitchel family was established at Nant

Cottage nearly three miles from the village of Bothwell. They were given almost two hundred acres of land to farm where they grew crops and reared a few sheep and cattle. 'Four hours every day,' Mitchel tells us 'were devoted to my three boys' lessons.' Farming was a lifestyle totally alien to him but he adapted with surprising ease and seemed outwardly content living in this 'thinly-peopled pastoral country with kind friends'. However, in a letter written to a friend in Ireland Mitchel comments, 'It would be uncandid to pretend that we are content or near to contentment here.'

Again in letter form, he paints a slightly different picture. Writing to John Blake Dillon who was now safely settled in America at the time Mitchel states:

> We are all in excellent health, and the climate is assuredly the best in the world. It has made a strong man of me, indeed far stronger than I ever was before, though I landed here worn to a shadow, and in fact, very nearly dead.

In *Jail Journal* (New Year's Day, 1853) he again writes favourably about life at Nant Cottage and his farming lifestyle:

> Of literature I am almost sick, and prefer farming, and making market of my wool. There is something stupefying to the brain, as well as invigorating to the frame in this genial clime and aromatic air.

The climate in Van Diemen's Land certainly agreed with Mitchel and there are no references to the 'asthma demon' during his stay there.

Early in 1853 Pat Smyth, an old school friend of Francis Meagher at Clongowes Wood Jesuit College, was sent to Tasmania to plan and assist in the escape bid of John Mitchel and William Smith O'Brien. Pat or P J Smyth was a member of Young Ireland and a member of the Irish Confederation. He had been commissioned by the Irish Directory in New York for this daring operation. Smyth, again through the Directory, had successfully planned the escape bids of Meagher and Terence McManus the previous year so he knew the ropes and the terrain.

As Smith O'Brien's sentence was for life, Mitchel and Pat

Smyth tried to persuade him that he should be first to avail of any opportunity of escape. O'Brien, however, was adamant that Mitchel should be given the chance and on this he would not be swayed. Mitchel realised that O'Brien was not going to change his mind and he agreed he would attempt the escape. For security reasons, including the arrest of Smyth in a case of mistaken identity, the escape bid was deferred for several months. Ironically, at one stage, the police arrested Smith believing him to be Mitchel. Also Smith had fallen seriously ill and this further delayed their plans.

In June of that year Mitchel resigned his 'ticket of leave' by walking into the police-magistrate's office, in the company of P J Smyth, and handing the official a note dated 8th June 1853. It stated simply, 'Sir, I hereby resign my 'ticket-of-leave' and withdraw my parole.' (Both men we're informed in *Jail Journal* were armed with pistols.) No sooner done than they bade the astonished official, 'good morning' and dashed from the building before Mitchel could be arrested. Outside they mounted their horses and said, 'Adieu for evermore' to Bothwell. In a forest, some two miles from Bothwell, they exchanged horses and coats and parted company.

On the evening of 18th July, after some six weeks 'on the run', the fugitive Mitchel was safely on board the *Emma* and sailing out of Hobart bound for Sydney. Jenny and their six children were also aboard but made little contact with Mitchel who was travelling under the assumed name of Mr. Wright. On 2nd August, now on board the *Orkney Lass*, Mitchel – now Mr. Warren – was on his way to Tahiti arriving in the beautiful South Sea island three weeks later. He spent three happy weeks there and found the Tahitians 'a tall, well-made, graceful and lazy race' who made him feel most welcome.

On 13th September he was on the final stage of his journey to San Francisco on board an American vessel, the *Julia Ann*. On stepping on deck he tells us in *Jail Journal* that he immediately 'took off his hat in homage to the Stars and Stripes'. Pat Smyth had sorted out everything perfectly, and Jenny, with her six children, was reunited with her husband. At this stage there was no need for anonymity and he had become once again 'plain John Mitchel' travelling with his family. His entry for that date (13th September) concludes, 'I am surrounded by my family, all well; we are away before a fine breeze for San Francisco; my *Jail Journal* ends and my "Out-of-Jail Journal" begins'.

On 9th October 1853 the *Julia Ann* sailed in through the Golden Gate. John and Jenny Mitchel were totally overwhelmed by the reception they would receive in San Francisco. In a speech he made shortly after his arrival Mitchel informed his audience that he had 'commenced his novitiate in order to become an American citizen' declaring in time he would become a 'true and thorough American'. (Naturalization took five years) Before long, with P J Smyth, he went in search of his old comrade in exile, Terence Bellew McManus but discovered he had left San Francisco and was now living in San Jose some fifty miles away. Three weeks later, with Jenny

Terence Bellew McManus

and Pat Smyth, he tracked down McManus in San Jose and spent a relaxing few days 'talking of scenes old and new'.

Friends, old and new, tried in vain to persuade him to remain in San Francisco and resume his career in law but Mitchel had his heart set on going on to New York where his mother, two of his sisters and his brother William were anxiously awaiting him. He also felt that in New York he would be nearer home in Ireland. John Blake Dillon, Francis Meagher, Devin Reilly and other refugees from Ireland were also in New York and he dearly wished to renew these old acquaintances.

On the morning of 29th November 1853 the Mitchel family's sea-faring days were at least temporarily over when they sailed into New York. Among the very first to come on board to greet them was John's younger brother William and Francis Meagher. Instead of landing in New York the entire party slipped away by boat to Brooklyn where Mitchel's mother and sisters were in a house eagerly waiting to meet them.

After an emotional reunion with his mother, John Blake Dillon with his wife Ady headed an apparently endless procession of well-wishers from Ireland. A carnival atmosphere with bands playing and cheering crowds waving banners pervaded the New York night air until well after midnight. This would continue for the next three or four nights. And so John Mitchel, parole-breaker, escapee and now political refugee, was 'warmly welcomed to the land of liberty and made to feel good after my long captivity'. Again in his own words: 'There seemed no end to the societies, clubs, companies that made it a point to come and welcome me to their hospitable land.' John Mitchel was already smitten by America and her people.

## Chapter 13

# New Life in America

MITCHEL WAS ONLY FIVE weeks in New York before he had taken up writing again, founding his own weekly newspaper the *Citizen*. He was joined initially in the project by Francis Meagher and his brother William was charged with the printing aspect and ensuring that publication times were met. In the prospectus which preceded the first edition, dated 7th January 1854, Mitchel pointed out that Meagher and himself

> refuse to believe that, prostrate and broken as the Irish nation is now, the cause of Irish independence is utterly lost or that Irishmen in America can endure the thought of accepting the defeat which has driven them from the land of their fathers.

Their new weekly newspaper would therefore be conducted in accordance with their memories and aspirations and its message directed to all true Irishmen and Irishwomen now living in America.

The *Citizen* began well and soon had a circulation of over fifty thousand copies and, as expected, drew most of its readership from the fast growing Irish-American community. In the *Citizen* Mitchel first published his *Jail Journal* over a seven-month period (14th January to 19th August) before having it published in book form later that year, 1854. Francis Meagher's contribution appears to have been small and in Mitchel's words 'there was little service from his dashing pen'. He had, however, two very capable assistants in John Savage and John McClenahan, former members of Young Ireland. Both men had avoided arrest and escaped to America after the Young Ireland Rebellion.

By the time the fourth edition appeared, the *Citizen* was already creating controversy when Mitchel first aired his views on, what he saw as, the legitimacy of slavery. It seems an extraordinary subject to involve himself in so early in his life in America but prudence was never one of Mitchel's chosen virtues. He wasn't one to shy away from debate either. His stance on the slavery question may help explain why Meagher seemed to distance himself from the *Citizen* at such an early stage. It is also the case that Mitchel would have had little first hand knowledge of the divisive nature of the slavery debate and how deep-rooted feelings were. This didn't deter him however, as week after week he published articles in support of slavery and, at times, resorted to personal attacks on those who didn't share his views.

Writing in the *Citizen* in a direct appeal to his Irish readership, Mitchel makes his views on 'white supremacy' alarmingly clear.

Thomas Francis Meagher

He goes a step further by invoking 'God's plan for mankind' to reinforce a basically flawed argument:

> He would be a bad Irishman who voted for principles which jeopardised the present freedom of a nation of white men, for the vague forlorn hope of elevating blacks to a level which it is at least problematical whether God and Nature intended them.

Exiled from a land, peopled by a race who were, in every way but name, slaves to landlordism, this is an incredible statement. In so short a time, had he forgotten the second-class status his countrymen endured in their own homeland? Had he forgotten the ships which left Ireland during the Famine crammed with his countrymen? A people forced by Famine to render their service for a pittance in a land which was not their own.

New York was not particularly receptive to this type of Southern propaganda and Mitchel's outspoken views on slavery certainly weren't designed to increase the circulation of the *Citizen*. Needless to say they didn't. Furthermore, his pro-slavery convictions certainly weren't shared by his friend and journalistic colleague Meagher who would later align himself with the North in the American Civil War. John Savage, Mitchel's co-writer in the *Citizen*, would fight alongside Meagher on the Federal side.

Several years before the outbreak of Civil War Mitchel had prophetically written:

> There is a northern nation and a southern nation; and possibly it will come to this, that they must either peaceably separate, dividing the continent between them, or else one must conquer the other. For so far I do hope it will not come to this; but, if it does, I think all my sympathies would be with the South.

He had committed fully to the South and the pro-slavery lobby at an early stage in the long and bitter verbal conflict which preceded the Civil War.

John Martin, having learned the direction Mitchel had taken the *Citizen* on the slavery issue, was saddened. He wrote of his deep disappointment:

> I had seen how Mitchel excited the rage and grief of many thousands of his political friends against him by the course he took on the question of Negro slavery... I lost the confident hope I rested in him. I saw the power for writing and organising the Irish patriots was gone.

A couple of years later, writing to a close friend in Ireland who was also alarmed at his forthright views, Mitchel argued that the 'African Negro was born and bred to slavery and therefore to set him free was impossible'. Despite all the well-intentioned advice proffered by those closest to him, Mitchel would not budge from his entrenched position.

The direction of the *Citizen* had certainly changed from the ideals set out in the prospectus of reflecting the 'memories and aspirations' of two Irish nationalists 'driven from the land of their fathers'. The cause of Irish Independence was in a short space of time demoted to a secondary issue behind the Southern Confederacy cause. The whole Irish ethos of the paper was gradually being overshadowed by the great American debate on slavery and its circulation continued to decline. Controversy in normal circumstances might have helped increase sales, but the *Citizen* was way too prejudiced for its New York readership.

Mitchel did find time however to enter into a public debate in the *Citizen* with the archbishop of New York on the morality of armed force in Irish nationalism. His belief in the right of Irish nationalists to use physical force remained unchanged and he would defend that right in whatever forum or against whatever quarter. The debate was stormy and at times, personal, but there was never going to be a winner and the *Citizen* was the eventual looser. In Mitchel's own words, 'Archbishop '*Philo Veritas*' Hughes, with his pastoral crosier, drew away a few thousand readers.'

Mitchel's dynamic role in support of the South soon prompted an invitation from the Mayor of Richmond in Virginia for Mitchel to come on a visit. He gladly accepted and found he was greeted as an honoured guest and treated royally. So great an impression did he make on this visit that he was invited back to Richmond a month later to deliver the annual oration at the University of Virginia. He considered this one of the greatest honours and pleasures of his life – 'a bright picture which I hang up in the chambers of my memory.' His loyalty to the South had been reinforced.

In Virginia, Mitchel felt flattered that he was being honoured for saying the very things which in New York he had been denounced. He was also amazed that here 'in the Land of Liberty, a man was supposed to conceal unpopular opinions'. He wrote shortly after his visit to Virginia that he saw there, 'the luckiest, jolliest and freest negroes on the face of the earth'.

On this same enlightening visit he informs us that, 'he learned that the cause of Negro slavery is the cause of true philanthropy'. There can't have been too many who agreed entirely with this observation even in the southern heartland.

It is worth pointing out how much Mitchel's views on slavery differed from those of his old adversary Daniel O'Connell. In parliament O'Connell successfully campaigned for the abolition of slavery throughout the British Empire believing it to be universally wrong both morally and on humanitarian grounds. (In 1833 the British Government passed its own Abolition of Slavery Act.) O'Connell was one of the few European politicians who involved himself directly in the anti-slavery cause in America.

He even returned money, destined for the Repeal Association, to Irish-American allies because it was accompanied by arguments in favour of slavery. It was, to his eternal credit, a matter of principle and he was not prepared to trade his abolitionist convictions for financial gain.

'By their memories of Ireland,' O'Connell declared, 'Irish-Americans should love liberty, hate slavery, and treat the blacks as their brethren.' This was in stark contrast to Mitchel's belief.

This inevitably throws up the question, how much did O'Connell's abolitionist views influence Mitchel in forming his conflicting views? The whole slavery debate was relatively new to Mitchel so it is possible that he may have been swayed initially by O'Connell's strong opposition to slavery. What is certain is that Mitchel's pro-slavery position was greatly strengthened by his own robust and articulate defence of it. In other words, he was becoming more convinced of the righteousness of slavery the more vigorously he argued in its favour. What may have started out as an ill-conceived attempt to encourage debate on an important moral question had for Mitchel passed that point of no return. He was in too deeply and his single mindedness simply kept him digging.

Towards the end of 1854, despite his huge commitment to the *Citizen*, Mitchel still found time to edit an edition of the poems of Thomas Davis. The anthology, with its extensive biographical introduction, is an excellent tribute to a man whose writing and qualities he had greatly admired. 'The loss of this rare and noble man,' wrote Mitchel, 'has never been repaired, neither to his country nor to his friends.'

## Mitchel Moves South to Tennessee

Little over a year after founding the *Citizen*, Mitchel decided to abandon his newspaper work and pursue some dream he had to be a farmer again. Early in 1855 the family left New York and moved to Tucaleechee Cove, an empty corner of the Great Smoky Mountains in Tennessee – a southern state with strong pro-slavery leanings.

Writing to his sister Matilda at the time he remarked that farming was most unlikely to make him a rich man but it had 'emancipated him from the foolish nonsense of New York life'. Unfortunately much of 'the foolish nonsense' was of his own creation. The pace of life in New York probably appeared hectic to Mitchel and his desire to be free of it is understandable. Both Newry and Bothwell were a far cry from the frenetic pace of New York life.

When money became scarce, as was often the case, Mitchel left their log-home and went off on a more lucrative lecture tour, something he later confessed he derived very little pleasure from. After delivering a poorly attended lecture in Savannah in Georgia, Mitchel remarked that the people of that city had 'too good sense to go to lectures'. The one consolation that lecturing did afford was that it offered him the opportunity to travel and see many of the great sights and cities of America.

Within a year he had become disillusioned with farming and the family was on the move once again, this time to Knoxville, capital of East Tennessee. For a time he contemplated a return to the legal profession but after a short lecture tour, mainly in the South, he launched his second newspaper the *Southern Citizen* in October 1856. Mitchel himself described it as 'an organ of extreme southern sympathy'. He was supported in this new venture by the mayor of Knoxville and leading Confederate, Mayor William Swan. It is very likely that Swan, a wealthy businessman, provided most of the money to set up the paper. (Unlike farming, journalism was very much in Mitchel's bones.)

The *Southern Citizen* persistently attacked the slavery abolitionists and their Union allies in the North. It even went so far as to draw comparisons between the role of England in Ireland and that of the North's interference in the affairs of the South. Mitchel on occasions referred to the South as 'The Ireland of this great continent' – a comparison that is, frankly, difficult to fathom. He believed that the more progressive and industrial North was intent on imposing its will on an agricultural southern nation which preferred to retain its own distinctive way of life. The South, like Ireland, was fighting for the right to govern itself and there the comparison surely ends. The role of England in Ireland was surely more nefarious than a difference of opinion on a way of life

Mitchel soon became something of a celebrity in Knoxville and he built an impressive house on the leafy edge of town. He rather quirkily named his new home 'Nowhere Else'. Here with his family around him he lived a more settled life for over two years. On occasions 'Nowhere Else' opened its doors to exiles from Ireland and this gave Mitchel the opportunity to catch up on events from back home. When the Civil War came and

Knoxville's first Confederate volunteer group was mustered in 1861, they called themselves the 'Mitchel Guards'. This gives us a clear indication of the high regard Mitchel was held by the good citizens of Knoxville.

In a letter to an Irish friend who remonstrated with him about his frequent attacks on the abolition movement, Mitchel replied:

> I consider Negro slavery here the best state of existence for the Negro and the best for his master; and I consider that taken out of their brutal slavery in Africa and promoting them to a humane and reasonable slavery here is also good... All I want to impress upon you is that I honestly mean all that I say. You must not deny me this credit.

Always a devout believer in the right of free speech he wasn't so tolerant on the right to personal freedom. In the 'Land of Liberty' didn't slavery epitomise the denial of liberty not to mention being in breach of the American constitution?

His Irish friend, in the same letter, asked Mitchel why he felt he had to involve himself in the whole controversy at all to which Mitchel responded that it was his intention, when granted American citizenship, to live in the South. However, in those last two sentences above, we find him almost appealing for some form of approval for holding views he must have realised were anathema to most, if not all, of his Irish friends. He didn't, on the other hand, retract or attempt to tone down his intemperate rhetoric.

In the *Southern Citizen* he went further by advocating the reopening of the slave trade with Africa which had been abolished nearly fifty years before in 1808. This was an unbelievable appeal which enjoyed very little support even among committed Confederates. The selling of slaves continued legitimately in the Southern States right up to the end of the Civil War (1865) when it was officially abolished in all states within the Union. Sensationally, Mitchel would later offend the citizens of Washington by suggesting that they repeal the law which had abolished slave trading. To add insult to injury he was living in Washington at the time.

Living in the South, Mitchel must have been conscious of an anti-Irish, anti-Catholic sentiment which existed there. Indeed it existed almost everywhere in America in the mid-nineteenth century but was particularly strong in the South. For the most part, it was a reaction to massive Irish immigration and was orchestrated by a rather shady group called the 'Know-Nothings'. They were a secret organization officially known as the Order of the United Americans but received their more familiar title because whenever a member was asked about the 'Order' he would invariably reply, 'I know nothing'.

Whether Mitchel ever saw the irony in his support for the South, where the 'Know-Nothings' had their power base, is unclear. His sister Matilda once made an assertion to him in a letter that the Irish or 'at least the rebel Irish' were despised the world over to which he disdainfully replied, 'This is a very complete mistake of yours. It is for *not* being rebels the Irish are despised.'

His general support for the Confederates' cause and his forthright endorsement of the institution of slavery in particular, lost him several friends and followers at that time and is a major source of embarrassment for many of his admirers today. During all his years living in the South, Mitchel himself never owned any slaves but in 1854, Writing in the *Citizen*, he openly conceded:

> As for me, I would quite happily be in Alabama on a plantation well stocked with healthy Negro slaves

He later accepted that this frank admission 'swept off ten thousand readers (of the *Citizen*) at one blow.' Evidently the financial repercussion of his pro-slavery position was not going to deter the dissentient journalist from expressing his beliefs. Curiously, it is accepted that Mitchel's wife Jenny shared none of her husband's strong opinions. While living in the South, she was quite adamant that there would be no Negro servant girls in her home and insisted that she and her daughters did all household chores themselves. Jenny appears to have been boss on all domestic matters and this may explain why the Mitchels never owned slaves.

In the autumn of 1858, Mitchel received a visit from James Stephens. Along with John O'Mahony and Thomas Clarke Luby, Stephens was one of the three founding member of the Irish Republican Brotherhood. The IRB had been formed in Dublin earlier that year, on St. Patrick's Day. This secret, oath-bound organization pledged to establish an Irish Republic by whatever means necessary. The leadership believed that England would never concede self-government to Ireland because of 'force of argument'. England, they believed would only concede to 'the argument of force'. Though many in the Brotherhood had been members of Young Ireland, the origins of the IRB dated back to Tone and the United Irishmen. Unlike Young Ireland, the IRB was committed to revolution and was a more potent political movement.

James Stephens, who was recognised as the movement's leader, was on the first of two fund raising tours he made to America. He hoped Mitchel, through the columns of his newspaper, would call on Irish-America to provide much-needed finance for the Fenians, the name by which the IRB was known in America. Stephens also hoped Mitchel would allow his paper to be used to promote the ideals of the movement and possibly to encourage recruitment.

John O'Mahony from Co. Limerick and Michael Doheny from Co. Tipperary, both Young Irelanders, set up the IRB in America and chose to name it the Fenians. In time, the name Fenians which had been adopted by O'Mahony, a passionate Gaelic scholar (and a fine classics scholar), came to be used by the movement on both sides of the Atlantic. (In Celtic Mythology, the first Fenians or Na Fianna, were a band of fearless warriors loyal to the legendary giant Fionn mac Cumhail.)

Mitchel had never met Stephens before but knew something of his reputation as an organiser and militarist. He was also aware that Stephens had been a Young Irelander and that he had been wounded at Ballingarry. Mitchel, curiously, turned down Stephens' request for help but gave a personal donation of $50 – a substantial sum of money for someone of his means.

Stephens was probably unaware that Mitchel had little time for the Fenian Movement or he might not have made this direct approach. The movement, on the other hand, was very much in its infancy so Mitchel was perhaps premature in forming any opinion of it just yet. At that time much of his energy was taken up sponsoring a very different cause and Irish Nationalism was perhaps not his primary concern.

## Chapter 14

# Washington and Paris

TWO WEEKS AFTER THE visit from James Stephens, the Mitchel family had uprooted yet again and moved to Washington. Mitchel felt that the *Southern Citizen* might make a more useful contribution here where the Confederates' case was poorly and unsympathetically presented. He still believed that if the argument was properly articulated, hearts and minds could be won over. In Tennessee his readership was pro-Confederacy so he was in fact, preaching to the converted. It was certainly an audacious move bringing his particular 'gospel' to the Union capital. Unsurprisingly, the move proved an abject failure and their stay in Washington was short-lived and won few converts.

William Smith O'Brien, who had been pardoned by the British government in 1854 on condition that he did not return to Ireland, visited Mitchel in Washington in February 1859. Having his old friend stay with him meant he had a lot of influential visitors to his home including senators and members of the American government. It even afforded him the opportunity to meet with American President, James Buchanan. Importantly it gave him some respite from journalism, particularly the intensity of the slavery debate which was now dominating American political life. The whole Mitchel family found Smith O'Brien's all too short a visit, both memorable and a welcome diversion.

After Smith O'Brien's departure and with him, all the excitement and buzz of social activity, Mitchel again grew discontented and now felt he needed to be nearer Ireland. France

John Mitchel, Paris 1861

had just declared war on Austria and Mitchel hoped England would be drawn into the conflict and this might offer an opportunity for Ireland to at last organise an effective rebellion. The Fenian cause now seemed a more plausible and attractive proposition to the previously sceptical Mitchel. He discontinued the *Southern Citizen* and sold all the printing machinery and materials to raise the necessary money. His partner William Swan had of course to be paid off, and August 1859 saw Mitchel relocate to Paris.

Before he left for Paris Mitchel had published an edition of the poetry of James Clarence Mangan (1803-1849) whom he greatly admired and had worked with while editor of the *Nation* and the *United Irishman*. He also had published around this time, a second book entitled *The Last Conquest of Ireland (Perhaps)*. It is Mitchel's own vivid recollections of that thrilling period in Irish history with which his own name and fame are so closely associated. It tells the story of O'Connell and Repeal and the emergence of 'Young Ireland'. It also covers in great detail Mitchel's appraisal of the Great Famine and, of course, Britain's reluctance to seriously tackle it. Mitchel also shares with us his personal evaluation of the ill-fated 'Young Ireland' Rebellion of 1848.

*Last Conquest* has for many historians and students, set the tone for Famine analysis to the present day. In a radical evaluation Mitchel concluded:

> A million and a half of men, women and children were carefully, prudently and peacefully slain by the English Government. They died of hunger in the midst of abundance, which their own hands had created... The Almighty indeed, sent the potato blight, but the English created the Famine.

In Paris he embarked on a satirical exposition of government methods in Ireland entitled 'An Apology for the British Government in Ireland'. It is vintage Mitchel, engaging on his favourite subject, the British Empire – 'that great machine for exploiting nations'. With recurring sarcasm he describes that same empire as a fine:

> example and bulwark of liberty, a great Providential agency for humanising and civilising mankind ... a beacon to guide the nations through their darkness to a brighter future.

The British Empire was a topic on which he expounded effortlessly and endlessly and with absolute enmity.

At the time of the publication of 'Last Conquest' Mitchel had sailed again for New York. Shortly before he left Paris John Martin, whom he had not seen since the escape from Tasmania more than six years before, came to stay with him. For Mitchel, this was the undoubted highpoint of what was otherwise a disappointing stay in Paris. Nothing beneficial to the Irish cause had materialised, so his reason for moving to Paris proved fruitless.

At his mother's home in Brooklyn Mitchel picked up his two youngest daughters, Minnie and Isobel, and continued to his home in Washington. In May of that year, 1860, he took his final oath of American Citizenship pledging to support the government of the United States. His loyalty to that same government would shortly be severely tested. In Washington,

Mitchel decided to resume his practice of law but firstly he had to study American law before he could be permitted. Money, or the lack of it, once again became a problem and he was off again on a lecture tour. The unlikely prospect of returning to law disappeared.

Shortly after a rare family holiday spent at David's Island near New York, the Mitchel family was on their way back to France. This was to be a 'permanent' move as they took all their worldly possessions with them including a piano. The two eldest boys had secured employment in America, Johnny as a civil engineer in Alabama and James in the insurance business in Richmond, and didn't join the family in Paris. Mitchel's only source of income was his writing and he acted as Paris correspondent for two American papers, the *Irish American* and the Southern based *Charleston Mercury*. He also wrote regular articles for the *Dublin Irishman*, articles which he later described as 'trashy'.

In the summer of 1861 he had a second visit from Smith O'Brien and Mitchel describes how his 'little household idolised the man'. The meeting between the two close friends was much too short despite the fact that they, in Mitchel's words, 'never agree upon any question, save one'. We are not informed what the one question was, but we can only but guess it had to relate to getting England out of Ireland. During the visit Mitchel had this strange sense of foreboding, and believed O'Brien shared it, that this would be the last time the two of them would meet.

## Chapter 15

# American Civil War 1861-65

...but one of them would make war rather than let the nation survive, and the other would accept war rather than let it perish, and the war came.
—Abraham Lincoln, March, 1865

THE OUTBREAK OF THE American Civil War in April 1861 would have far-reaching consequences for John Mitchel and his family. As he had predicted several years before in the *Citizen*, relationships between the North and the South became so hostile that indeed 'one must conquer the other'. Abraham Lincoln, an outspoken opponent of slavery, was elected President and, rather than accept Lincoln as President, eleven states from the South, including Tennessee, broke away from the Union. Secession from the Union was preferable to abandoning slavery and their established values. They formed the Southern Confederacy with their own government and President based in Richmond.

Even with the prospect of a long and bloody civil war Mitchel's support for the South remained as rock-solid as ever. He held firm to his belief that there were two nations in America, with fundamentally different philosophies of life. Mitchel saw the Southern states as static and agricultural, refusing to sacrifice its traditional way of life on the land for industrial expansion and 'the pretensions of new-made wealth'. The Northern states, on the other hand, were going through the industrial revolution and were more dynamic, eager for wealth regardless of cost, and always seeking to expand. Mitchel felt that the South was expected to move from being an agricultural nation to being part of a much greater industrial nation against the inherent and legitimate wishes of its people.

Although the population in the North was growing, more people were desperately needed to work in the factories which were mushrooming in cities like New York, Chicago and Philadelphia. The North believed that if, granted their freedom, slaves would abandon the plantations in the South and provide the labour they urgently required. Mitchel contended that this was merely another form of exploitation and was slavery in everything but name. His argument couldn't be dismissed entirely. Indeed there was a great deal of truth in it.

It should be remembered that Mitchel had always been unimpressed by the rapid change to industrialism prevalent in the mid 19th-century and this is why he felt more comfortable living in the South. While most of his contemporaries welcomed new inventions in manufacturing and communications Mitchel remained sceptical. He was unconvinced that there were any 'real advantages' achieved through the advances in science and technology. In fact he found it 'absurd, this triumphant glorification of the current century upon being the century it is'. He certainly couldn't be accused of being too progressive in outlook.

Mitchel also found it offensive that the current century, in his words, 'took pride in itself and sneered at the wisdom of its ancestors'. This recent phenomenon, he claimed, 'indicated not higher wisdom but deeper stupidity'. His contempt for modernism was possibly rooted in what he described as his 'diseased and monomaniacal hatred' of the power and materialism which he associated with Victorian Britain – a nation 'which proclaimed itself as the vanguard of 19th century progress'. In short, his hatred of Britain and his hatred of progress probably fed of each other.

Mitchel believed that those who argued in favour of the abolition of slavery and were critical of him, hadn't given full consideration to the facts. His pro-slavery position is well documented but, in Mitchel's defence, was not always quoted in its full context. He argued that the Negro slave, 'owned by an honourable and Christian master', was better off than the wage slaves working in the factories of New York and Chicago or the consumptive seamstresses working in Northern sweatshops.

Working conditions in factories in northern cities may well have been akin to 'slave labour' but the question of equality between black and white was unfortunately overlooked in Mitchel's judgement. He seems to have disregarded the whole moral question of ownership as well. Surely it is unchristian and therefore unacceptable, for one human being to own another. It was justifiable however in Mitchel's hypothesis if the slaves' master was honourable and God-fearing.

He also seemed to regard the slaveholder as a sort of legal guardian or 'father of an extended family' with certain responsibilities for his slaves' social and moral welfare.

There is little doubt that he considered the Negro intellectually inferior to members of the white race and in need of moral guidance. Laws in the South certainly did nothing to disprove Mitchel's claim as in most states it was illegal to teach slaves to read or write. The moral issue is even more startling when we're reminded that the rape of female slaves was not considered illegal except if it represented trespassing on another man's 'property'.

As far back as 1854, before he had moved to the South, Mitchel claimed that it was neither a crime nor morally wrong to flog slaves. Writing in the *Citizen* he shares with us his views on the physical maltreatment of black slaves. He wrote at that time:

> We deny that it is a crime, or a wrong, or a peccadillo, to hold slaves, to buy slaves, to keep slaves at their work by flogging or other needful coercion...

Life on a southern plantation was extremely harsh for black slaves and punishment was meted out quite mercilessly and at the absolute discretion of the slave owner.

When war began in April 1861, Mitchel was living with his family in Paris. The uncertainty and concern for his sons' safety, dictated that he should return again to America. Both sons were now in their early twenties and had enlisted in the Confederate States' Army. Johnny was the first foreign-born officer to receive a commission in the army of South Carolina. This, the state authorities said, was in tribute to his father's 'principled stand' as a leading Confederate propagandist. James had joined as a private in the 1st Virginia Infantry, but he too was soon given promotion and a commission.

On arrival in America in September 1862, Mitchel and his youngest son Willie immediately made their way south to the state of Virginia. Willie was just eighteen years old and had been attending university in Paris before returning to America. Firstly father and son had to penetrate a Union blockade before reaching Richmond. Here Mitchel presented himself to Jefferson Davis, a former state senator and now President of the Confederate States. Willie enlisted in the same regiment as his brother James, 1st Virginia Infantry. All three sons were now, as their father expressed it, 'on the rough edge of battle'

Mitchel himself joined Richmond City Guard and an Ambulance Corps where he tended the wounded and helped transfer them to military hospitals. He was disqualified for active military service on health grounds including his poor eyesight.

Writing to his wife Jenny who had followed him to America, Mitchel describes the dreadful conditions the medics were forced to endure:

> We are here in the midst of a scene of horror and anguish and filth, receiving the wounded and putting them on board trains. Half of us up and working all night all of us busily engaged all day. I cannot yet guess when we may get away and go home. We sleep on the ground under tents.

His term with the Confederate ambulance corps was probably brief and it was with the pen that Mitchel rendered best service to his adopted cause. In addition to war duties he edited a daily newspaper, *The Richmond Enquirer* which was favourable to President Davis and his administration. However, the rival Richmond daily, the *Examiner*, although naturally favourable to the Confederacy, was very critical of the President and what they saw as his weak handling of the war.

Mitchel too, was beginning to find fault with the President's policy, believing he was neither decisive enough nor ruthless enough to win the war. Early in 1863 he resigned the editorship of the *Enquirer* and joined the more radical *Examiner*. The editorials in the *Examiner* now reflected Mitchel's view that the President was 'too slack and timid in enforcing upon the Federal Army due respect for the laws of war by an unrelenting course of retaliation.'

That same year Mitchel acquired a large house in 5th Street, Richmond, and settled down again to something like family life, if that was possible, in the war-torn South. Only two of his six children, Minnie and Isobel, shared the family home as all three sons were away from home at war and Henrietta was in Paris. Despite the uncertainty of the war Mitchel's life had, for the first time in a long time, some semblance of order about it. But all of this would be short-lived.

In the summer of that year he was to receive the heartbreaking news from Paris that Henrietta, their eldest daughter, had died at her convent school, Sacre Coeur, in Paris. For Mitchel and Jenny it was the first break in their family of six. Henrietta had joined the Sisters of the Sacred Heart only two years before and was well beloved by young and old within the convent community. Her father voiced no objections when she told him she wished to become a Catholic. For him it was 'a matter of private judgement', something he had learned from his father, and he respected Henrietta's right to make her own judgement.

About Henrietta's change of faith her father wrote:

> I knew that she was greatly influenced by her very strong Irish feeling, and had a kind of sentiment that one cannot be thoroughly Irish without being a Catholic.

He also tells us that 'connections in the North of Ireland wrote to me urging that I ought to exert my authority to stop such an apostasy.' Yet, he steadfastly defended his decision not to interfere in what he believed was a matter for personal conscience. In loving terms he wrote of Henrietta's change of faith:

> Here was a girl of nineteen, full of intelligence and spirit, gentle and affectionate, who never gave her father or mother one moment's uneasiness, deliberately declaring that she desired to embrace the ancient faith of her forefathers.

Mitchel informs us that his mother expressed her fears that he too was contemplating embracing Catholicism but he assured her that her worries were unfounded. His own faith was something Mitchel rarely wrote or spoke about but loyalty to his father's memory and ministry would, for him, always forbid 'such apostasy'. He seemed to regard religion with a degree of cynicism and once described himself as 'an unworthy member of the pagan persuasion'. How much of the sentiment that 'one cannot be thoroughly Irish without being a Catholic' which he attributed to Henrietta, was in fact shared by Mitchel himself, we will never know!

The remains of Henrietta Mitchel lie at peace in the cemetery of Mont Parnasse in Paris. It was a place where her devoted father often brought flowers and was seen standing deep in thought, while working in the French capital in 1865-66.

Henrietta's sudden death was the first of a double tragedy which would befall the Mitchel family in a matter of a few months. Less than a year after enlisting 'Little Billy' (a term of endearment Mitchel used) was fatally wounded at Gettysburg in July 1863. He had been on summer leave and had walked well over one hundred miles to rejoin his regiment in Pennsylvania only days before his death.

Private Willie Mitchel was one of nearly four thousand Confederate infantry slaughtered in Pickett's ill-fated charge on 3rd July 1863. Over three thousand Federal soldiers also died in the three days of carnage in what was the bloodiest battle of the war. They blindly followed orders and charged to certain death. Billy was one of the flag bearers of his regiment, Virginia's 1st Infantry.

His grief-stricken father wrote at the time, 'He could not have fallen in better company or, as I think, in a better cause.' But how much did the nineteen year old flag bearer understand of that 'just and noble cause' for which he sacrificed his life? It was all a far cry from the carefree, student life at university in Paris. To his eldest son Johnny, Mitchel wrote some weeks later, 'So poor Billy finished his first and last campaign.' To his father, Willie or 'Little Billy' was little more than a boy and the nature of his death surely compounded his grief.

All that Mitchel ever saw again of his youngest son was a notebook filled with detailed notes and drawings of insects Billy had made. A comrade and fellow countryman, Captain John Dooley, who was with Willie when he died, had forwarded this beautiful memento to his grieving parents in Richmond. Billy and his tiny box of insects were apparently, inseparable. Captain Dooley, who assumed the role of older brother to Billy, wrote fondly in his diary of Billy's 'relentless pursuit of the intricacies of the special mini-life of bugs, beetles, butterflies and bees'. Unlike his older brothers, Willie Mitchel was a most unlikely candidate for soldiering.

Reportedly, a Confederate soldier found Billy's body and wrapped it in his army war blanket. He fastened the blanket with three large pins and attached a note to one of them. It simply read, 'Private William Mitchel, son of the Irish patriot.' The Irish Confederate boy, who innocently wanted to be a soldier like his two older brothers but couldn't harm a fly, sadly lies in an unmarked grave in Gettysburg, Pennsylvania.

Exactly a year later, on 20th July 1864, while working in the *Richmond Examiner* office, a telegram was brought informing Mitchel that his eldest son Johnny had been killed in action. He had died heroically defending Fort Sumter in South Carolina where he was commanding officer. Ironically, Johnny had played a key role back in April 1861 in the bombardment and eventual capture of Fort Sumter which was then held by Union forces. This was the opening military engagement of the Civil War. Captain John C Mitchel was described by a fellow officer as 'a born soldier, a man of nerve, finely tempered as steel, with habits of order, quick perception and decision, and he had been earnestly recommended for promotion.'

He was twenty-six years old when he was killed and the telegram which informed his father of his death stated that 'this country has been deprived of one of its most valuable defenders'. John C Mitchel was buried in Magnolia Cemetery in Charleston, South Carolina. A granite monument erected later by his comrades in the 1st Regiment, South Carolina Artillery bears the inscription:

> 'I willingly give up my life for South Carolina. Oh, that I could have died for Ireland!' – *His Last Words.*

The grave is surrounded by a replica of the parapet at Fort Sumter upon which Johnny Mitchel bravely gave his life.

Mitchel's third son, Captain James Mitchel, became chief of staff to General Gordon. He was seriously wounded and lost an arm, at the Battle of Chancellorsville in Virginia, in May 1863. He was able to return to duty after several months leave and was appointed to a staff position in the Confederate War Office in Richmond. James was Mitchel's only son to survive the war but he suffered much more than the loss of a limb. The mental scars he would take with him to the grave.

Clearly broken hearted, but never a man to wear his heart on his sleeve, Mitchel now immersed himself totally in his work. Into his writing he put every shred of passion and fanaticism of which he could muster. Often he drew parallels with Irish history pointing out why one nation cannot allow itself to be subjugated by another. He warned, he pleaded, and he used all his powers of persuasion to convince his readers why the South cannot allow itself to be defeated.

There was an element of desperation creeping into his writing as the war turned more and more against the South.

He prophetically warned:

> Failure will compel us to drink the cup of humiliation, even to the bitter dregs of having the history of our struggle written by New England historians.

The American Civil War finally came to an end in April 1865 when General Robert E Lee's Confederate Army surrendered and Richmond fell to the Federal Army. The cause to which Mitchel had sacrificed two of his three sons had failed utterly. Over 600,000 soldiers had died and slavery was finally abolished in what had been the Confederate States. Now there was truly only one nation to survive.

For Mitchel's only surviving son, failure and the awful consequences of failure were a bitter experience and his father had great difficulty persuading him to remain in America. The South, to James, now felt like a country under occupation and he stayed on in Richmond for the family's sake only. As the sole remaining son he was now closer than ever to his father and they were both becoming more dependent on each other. Sadly for James, the war was not to be the last of his personal heartbreak. Maybe his father's description of the South as being 'the Ireland of this great continent' had now a truer ring to it. Like his father had warned, James also found 'the cup of humiliation' a bitter draught to swallow.

In a letter written to a friend in Ireland some months after the war ended, we find one of Mitchel's rare references to his own personal and irreparable loss. He wrote:

> We have suffered heavily indeed, one way and another, by that Confederate business, and although it was a good cause, I must admit I grudge it what it has cost us – the lives of our two sons in defence of a country which, after all, was not their own.

He never seemed to waver in his views, never retracted a single word, even when it brought immense personal tragedy, but a man like Mitchel, who loved his family deeply, must have experienced grave doubts. He had committed himself so early and so fully to the Southern cause that there was no going back. He appeared unconcerned by all the well-intentioned protest and, if anything it merely strengthened his resolve. Outwardly he sounded convinced of the righteousness of the Confederates' cause but he must have seriously tortured his brain convincing himself that he was right to champion it. The dire consequences in the end must surely have outweighed any profound conviction.

The Southern States were ravaged and its people beggared by an unnecessary and bloody war. With the death of his daughter Henrietta in France, the Mitchel family was reduced to half of what it was in little over a year. Personal resources were also greatly reduced as a result of the war and so Mitchel decided to go to New York in search of work. He soon found employment becoming editor of the New York *Daily News*, a paper with Southern sympathies. Mitchel tells us that he feared for his personal safety in New York and that the more extreme Yankee newspapers called for his immediate silencing and arrest.

Nevertheless, he at once set himself the task of justifying the Confederates' cause to an unreceptive readership, and, at the same time appealing to the North to show compassion for the vanquished. He also called for the North to do all in their power to heal the deep divisions which still existed after the war and which the North, in Mitchel's view, still fomented. Regardless of what we may think of Mitchel's loyalties, railing against the Union, in Northern heartland, after the Union victory, took a lot of nerve. No one could ever accuse him of not having the courage of his convictions, but you could question his judgement of where and when to express it. He just seemed incapable of controlling his deep-rooted feelings regarding 'that whole unfortunate Confederacy business'.

It was certainly not the type of sentiment that New York or Washington wished to hear and resentment against him continued to grow, mainly within the Pro-Union press. Editorials called on the government to suppress Mitchel's views often attributing to him offensive articles which he neither penned nor approved of. He was arrested on the orders of General Ulysses Grant on 14th June and immediately shipped to Fortress Monroe, a remote military prison in Virginia. Three days later he was locked up without charge or trial, now a prisoner of the American, or Yankee as Mitchel preferred to call it, Government. He was to be kept an isolated prisoner and was not to be allowed communicate with anyone.

Sometime later Mitchel wrote of the irony of his imprisonment. He mused that at least the British government, with their dismissive attitude to justice in Ireland, had passed a spurious Act of Parliament to imprison him; the American Government threw him into jail without the 'pretence of law, trial or accusation'. He also boasted that he was the only person in the world who could claim to have been

> prisoner-of-state to the British and American Governments one after the other. And these two governments, we are told, are the very highest expression and grandest hope of the civilisation of the 19th century.

Writing to a friend after his release, Mitchel joked that had he stayed long enough in France he would doubtless have been locked up there also.

Before Mitchel's arrival in Fortress Monroe the Union Army held only two prisoners on general charges of war crime – Jefferson Davis and Senator Clement Clay of Alabama. In all likelihood the Confederate President and his most loyal propagandist enjoyed little contact. Mitchel doesn't seem to allude to it in his writings.

Initially he was kept in solitary confinement, denied access to books or exercise and treated harshly by his gaolers. His old enemy asthma became, once more, a nightly visitor and he got little sleep. Medical staff in the prison became concerned about his health and after two months he was allowed daily exercise and was given a much improved diet. He was experiencing respiratory problems and there was the real fear that he was in the early stages of tuberculosis.

Mitchel was imprisoned for four months and his eventual

release was largely due to the political influence the Fenian Movement was able to exert in America at that time. Interestingly, the vast majority of the American Fenians had served with the Union Army during the Civil War and had obviously set aside past differences to help secure his release. This fact also serves to remind us of the high standing Mitchel still held in Irish-American circles that past differences could be ignored in his case.

Fortress Monroe had seriously damaged Mitchel's health and, although only days short of his fiftieth birthday at the time of his release on 30th October, he now resembled a man of much greater age. Imprisonment had also taken a serious toll on Mitchel's spirit and he worried more about his duty to his family and their general welfare. Prison had given him a lot of time to think but he remained as resolute as ever regarding the Confederacy cause.

It is interesting to know whether Mitchel's treatment in Fort Monroe altered his views on prison conditions generally and indeed, on capital punishment. In an entry in *Jail Journal* dated 3rd Feb. 1849, he gives vent to his feelings on both issues. He argued that

> Jails ought to be places of discomfort and the 'sanitary condition' of miscreants ought not to be better cared for than honest, industrious people – and for 'ventilation', I would ventilate the rascals in front of the county jails at the end of a rope.

The jocular, almost tongue-in-cheek language he uses makes us wonder how serious Mitchel was when he wrote this. It should also be pointed out that he recorded these comments while on board the *Dromedary* in the company of several hundred 'common' criminals with whom, on his admission, he had little or no contact. The facetious nature of his observations may have been for Mitchel's own amusement and perhaps weren't meant to be taken literally or even read by the greater public.

He seems a lot more serious however, when he attacks in the same entry those who campaigned for prison reform. They are being *'sadly retrogressive'* and he insists, with typical candour, that they:

> have no right to make the honest support the rogues, and support them better than they, the honest people, can support themselves. You have no right to set a premium upon villainy and put burglars and rickburners on a permanent endowment.

Without the gallows and the guillotine, Mitchel further claimed, 'this planet would be uninhabitable.'

These seemingly extreme views must be viewed in the context of their time, the mid 19th century. At that time capital punishment was very common and was widely accepted as the ultimate deterrent. Indeed, friends and associates of Mitchel had received the death penalty and fortunately had their sentence commuted. Their crimes were of a political nature and sentence had been handed down by a 'corrupt and illegal justice system'. His opinion on prison conditions however, was scarcely accurate, as jails in the mid-nineteenth century were places of dire discomfort and in urgent need of improvement. To demand an upgrading in sanitation, diet, accommodation etc. was scarcely a retrogressive move.

Among the few letters he received while in Fort Munroe was one from Newry telling him of his mother's death. She had returned to Ireland with her daughters while her son was living in Richmond. Shortly before the Civil War had ended she had died in her home at Dromolane. It was another sore blow for an emotionally bruised and battered but unbowed John Mitchel.

## Chapter 16

# Mitchel and Fenianism

SHORTLY AFTER HIS RELEASE from Fort Monroe, Mitchel joined his family in Richmond before returning again to New York. Here he was approached by senior members of the Fenian Brotherhood and asked to join. There had always been uneasiness between Mitchel and the Fenians going back to James Stephens' visit in 1858 but he was nevertheless won over. It was well known, even within the brotherhood, that Mitchel had serious misgivings about 'secret organisations' but they succeeded in convincing him that their prospects for success were good. Perhaps he felt he was in some way indebted to the movement for helping secure his release from Fort Monroe.

Having joined, the leadership immediately appointed him as their financial agent in Paris. They had chosen their man wisely – he was a fluent French speaker and, more importantly, was scrupulously honest. On 10th November, 1865, Mitchel sailed out of New York for France. Before his departure he went to Washington and surrendered his certificate of naturalization which qualified him for American citizenship. The Civil War and its aftermath had left him completely disillusioned and he would no longer doff his hat 'in homage to the Stars and Stripes'.

He arrived in Paris on 23rd November and immediately took up his fiscal duties. Large sums of money passed through his hands while in Paris and though still suffering ill effects from his recent imprisonment he discharged his duties thoroughly. He kept meticulous ledgers of all monies received and paid out, but he wasn't informed – nor was there any records kept – of how these funds were being used. Soon he was having serious worries about how these sums were being appropriated. After serving approximately seven months in his position, he resigned and severed his links with the Fenians. He never seemed to be at ease within the organisation and always had grave reservations about certain aspects of it. He was, however, still fully committed to the aims and aspirations of Fenianism.

Prior to Mitchel's departure, James Stephens had taken over from John O'Mahony as leader of the Fenian Movement in America as well as in Ireland. Mitchel had written to O'Mahony in April seeking confirmation that Stephens would not be instated as head of the brotherhood in America. Mitchel also stressed that he earnestly hoped this was not their intentions but it is unclear what his main objections were. John O'Mahony was probably one of the few within the movement whom Mitchel really trusted but there seemed always to be animosity between himself and James Stephens.

In September 1865 the government moved against the Fenians by suppressing the *Irish People* a paper founded by Stephens to spread Fenian ideals. Mitchel believed that the organization in Ireland had by now become heavily infiltrated by British agents and Stephens had left it much too late to call a rising. Stephens had confidently predicted that 1865 would be the year of rebellion but the months passed by without the order to rise. Stephens believed that more support, in the form of arms and men, would come from America and 1866 then became the year.

Meanwhile the government continued to pick up leading Fenians and sentence them to long terms of imprisonment. O'Donovan Rossa and John O'Leary were arrested in 1865 and sentenced to twenty years penal servitude. John Devoy, arrested in February 1866, received fifteen years. Stephens was arrested in November 1865 but managed to escape two weeks later due largely to the efforts of John Devoy.

In a letter dated 9th January 1866, Stephens informed Mitchel that nearly one-third of the British Army in Ireland were

Fenians but now these regiments with Fenians in them were being moved out of Ireland to the colonies. But still Stephens hesitated and the movement was beginning to disintegrate, with morale at an all-time low. While Stephen procrastinated, mistrust in his leadership grew.

Mitchel had written to O'Mahony in March 1866 about the arrests in Ireland and voiced his concern about the whole internal security of the organization. In this letter he wrote:

> This prompt action of the English Government was precisely what they (the Fenian leadership) ought to have expected; what they ought to have been prepared for; what they ought to have anticipated by striking two months ago, if they were to strike at all.

In the same letter he also informed O'Mahony that he was having severe doubts about remaining as the movement's financial agent in Paris. Not surprisingly, he resigned approximately two months later. He certainly didn't commit as fully to the Fenian cause as he did to other causes and was always a reluctant recruit.

Stephens was deposed as leader, both in Ireland and America, in December of that year (1866) and left the brotherhood with his reputation irreparably damaged. The American Fenians denounced him as a 'rogue, imposter and a traitor' but to be fair to Stephens much of the criticism levelled against him was unwarranted. He was replaced by Thomas Kelly, a former colonel in the Federal Army during the Civil War. His appointment as leader can't have pleased Mitchel either but most Civil War veterans, recruited to Fenianism, had fought on the Northern side.

The American brotherhood in particular seemed to be overly critical of Stephens' delaying tactics and believed a more militant leadership was needed. Maybe it was a case of patriotism and martyrdom seeming more attractive the further we are removed from our native land. The American leadership clearly felt that the reputation of the movement was being eroded the longer a rising was delayed. Stephens believed that if insurrection in Ireland was to stand any chance of success,

James Stephens

England must simultaneously be engaged in war with one of the 'Great Powers'. Like many in Young Ireland before him, he wasn't prepared to risk annihilation in a 'lost cause' or simply to placate the American wing. Interestingly, it had been a long standing conviction of Mitchel that Ireland's opportunity would only come when England was engaged in war elsewhere.

A rising was planned for 6th March 1867 and, though large in numbers, the rebels were poorly armed and unprepared and were easily defeated. On the eve of the planned rising a blizzard settled down over the entire country bringing the heaviest snowfall in years. An insurrection in such adverse conditions was unthinkable but the order to rise couldn't be countermanded. In all, about twelve insurgents were killed in the Rising and hundreds were arrested and sentenced to long terms in English gaols where they were treated barbarically. In the space of two years, seven Fenians died in English gaols and another four died by their own hand. Many would lose their sanity and emerged after lengthy sentences as feeble, prematurely aged men.

On a near starvation diet of bread, water and porridge prisoners were forced to do the hardest labour in all weathers. No exception was made for prisoners like Charles Kickham, novelist and editor of the *Irish People*. Although deaf and nearly blind, he was made work outside in the depths of winter like his Fenian brothers. The diabolical treatment meted out to O'Donovan Rossa, is well documented where he was forced to live for periods of up to thirty days with his hands manacled behind his back. The manacles weren't always removed at night to allow him sleep and they were only changed to the front to allow him to eat twice daily. The squalid conditions Fenian prisoners were forced to endure were inhuman. To add to their other sufferings they were subjected daily to the vilest insults and taunts from their gaolers and hardened English convicts.

The public execution of the 'Manchester Martyrs', William Allen, Michael Larkin and Michael O'Brien, in Salford Prison on 23rd November 1867, caused an international outcry even among those bitterly opposed to Fenianism. Notably, the Catholic clergy shifted its attitude which had previously been hostile to one of tacit approval. Many priests identified with the great public display of mourning but the hierarchy was not quite so supportive. Cardinal Paul Cullen, head of the Catholic Church in Ireland, and the bishop of Kerry, David Moriarty, were bitter opponents. The Kerry prelate went so far in his condemnation to suggest that 'Eternity was not long enough nor Hell hot enough for Fenian members.'

The failure of the insurgents possibly vindicated Mitchel's assessment that the opportunity for a successful Rising had long passed as the surprise element no longer existed. Regarding the infiltration of the movement, it is true that the government seemed to have no difficulty identifying who the leaders were and were able to arrest them. The high level of recruitment, by its very nature, rendered secrecy virtually impossible and informers were able to get too close to the leadership.

After the Fenian Rising, the Republican tradition was never in danger of dying out completely. Following the amnesty of

1871, Fenian leaders like John Devoy and Jeremiah O'Donovan Rossa went to America and joined a new 'Fenian-type' movement called Clan na Gael. Its aims were to promote, in all ways possible, the cause of Irish Nationalism and ensure that the 'Irish Question' remained centre stage with Irish-Americans. Clan na Gael became a major fund raising body for Irish Republicanism and maintained a significant input in directing Irish political life for almost half a century.

The Fenian legacy was spelt out clearly for us by Pearse at the graveside of O'Donovan Rossa. At the end of his funeral oration delivered in August 1915, Pearse warned the British of what this legacy meant:

> Life springs from death, and from the graves of patriot men and women spring living nations...; but the fools, the fools, the fools – they have left us our Fenian dead, and while Ireland holds these graves, Ireland unfree shall never be at peace.

O'Donovan Rossa had gone to New York after his release from prison in 1871, and he died there in June 1915. His body was brought home to Ireland for burial in Glasnevin Cemetery.

It is popularly acknowledged that Mitchel had a problem with Stephens and seemed to doubt his sincerity and his motives. However, the authority which Stephens exerted within the movement had seriously dwindled by the time of Mitchel's departure so that can't have been his sole reason. He was disheartened by dissension among the leadership in America, one faction even wanting to invade Canada in order to stir up hostilities between the United States and Britain, and this may have been a factor. He was of course convinced that the time was no longer right for armed rebellion and the movement simply didn't have a future.

The fact that the Fenian Movement was a secret organization, and Mitchel made well-known his views on such organizations, unquestionably influenced his decision to quit. He believed that because of the 'supposed secrecy of their conspiracy', they were more likely to be of interest to the British authorities and open to infiltration by spies or informers. It is an interesting theory with probably more than a grain of truth. But what was the alternative – prepare for armed insurrection openly? Recall Mitchel's open invitation to Lord Clarendon to place a Castle spy in the offices of the *United Irishman* (April 1848).

It is probably true to say that Mitchel's sympathy was more for the spirit of Fenianism rather than the actual movement itself. The length of his tenure in the Fenians would indicate this. It was also known that he had little time for cliques and factions and they were rife in the organisation. Against his personal judgement, he allowed himself to be pressurised into joining the brotherhood so it was never going to be an enduring alliance. He may also have felt uncomfortable working with so many veterans of the American Civil War who had fought on the Union side. It was nearly twenty years since Mitchel had been involved directly in Irish Nationalism and the fiery enthusiasm may not have burned so vigorously.

While working on his *History of Ireland* the following year Mitchel was asked to accept the Presidency of the Fenians. It was hoped that he could unite the various factions within the movement but he flatly declined. He also refused to join in any appeal to his countrymen in America to contribute more money to a movement, which in his opinion, no longer offered any chance of success. 'It is wasting their means,' he wrote 'and what is worse it is wasting and using up their patriotic enthusiasm.' He confided to John Martin that, had he accepted the leadership, he would have been compelled to make radical, unpopular and sweeping changes to the organization.

Later he expressed similar views publicly and this deeply offended many Irish-American politicians as well as a great number of sincere patriots, both in Ireland and America, who still supported the main aims, spirit and strategy of the Fenian Brotherhood.

Mitchel spent little over a year in France and overall, it had not been a happy time. After severing his links with the Fenians he resumed his work in freelance journalism and in a letter to

Jenny he poured his heart out. In it he wrote:

> I am a lonely wretch and very little can give me pleasure except to hear about my own folk. I have been twice to the theatre since I came and both times quitted it before the piece was finished. Books are still some source ...

It is true that his visits to the great libraries of Paris helped fill up his time and lift his mind but his stay in Paris was a major disappointment. His heart was simply never in his work with the Fenians and he missed his family greatly. The loneliness must also have brought with it terrible memories of the Civil War.

In September, 1866, his two closest friends John Martin and Fr. Kenyon visited him and this temporarily raised his spirits. Mitchel wrote of their time together:

> We passed several days in and around Paris, we three, but with an occasional sad feeling that the three, John Kenyon, John Martin and John Mitchel might probably never meet again.

Mitchel left Paris at the close of that year and returned to the United States. He would never again revisit France or place flowers – 'laurustinus in a large pot' – on Henrietta's tombstone in the cemetery of Mont Parnasse.

## Chapter 17

# The *Irish Citizen*

IN 1867 MITCHEL RETURNED to New York and soon picked up where he left off in journalism. He founded, with his son James, his third newspaper in America. The word *Citizen* was retained in the title and Mitchel called it simply the *Irish Citizen*. It was a weekly publication, pro- Democratic Party, and continually criticised President Grant's policies towards the South. Mitchel still felt that, though the war had ended almost three years previously, Northerners continued to be vindictive and unjust in their treatment of the South. He seemed to feel that certain issues still needed to be highlighted and he was duty-bound to bring them to the public's attention. He wouldn't or couldn't move on but for someone with Mitchel's personal involvement it can't have been easy to lay the past to rest. Perhaps it was no longer the North that he was trying so desperately to convince but himself.

The *Irish Citizen* got off on the wrong foot with the more radical Irish/Americans. Contrary to their expectations, Mitchel declined to support the Fenian cause. He infuriated them even further by suggesting that they should pledge their allegiance solely to their adopted country, America. At the time Mitchel would have been a leading figure in America within the pro-Nationalist Irish, and his stand on Fenianism would have been a major disappointment to his supporters.

Through the columns of the *Irish Citizen* he often turned his attention to Ireland and the Home Government Association founded by Isaac Butt in 1870. The Association had been founded to demand some form of 'Home Rule' for Ireland with limited powers, while maintaining the link with Britain. Prime Minister Gladstone had recently introduced reforms, namely the Land Act and the Disestablishment of the Church of Ireland Act, but these reforms were felt to be insufficient. As a result, the Home Government Association was formed to demand an Irish Parliament.

Isaac Butt was a native of Co. Donegal and a brilliant barrister who had defended many of Fenian leaders, most of whom could not afford to pay him. Like Mitchel he was the son of a clergyman and both had attended Trinity College about the same time. Unlike Mitchel, Butt was initially pro the Act of Union but the Famine was to change all that and he came to support Repeal and defended a number of the Young Irelanders in court.

In the *Irish Citizen* Mitchel frequently criticised the aims and tactics of the Home Government Association, believing it didn't go far enough. Its demand for a Dublin Parliament without sovereignty was totally unsatisfactory to Mitchel. Remember, this was the man who twenty five years previously felt Repeal was no longer an option. He wasn't about to hail Home Rule without total separation as a feasible alternative.

Three years after its formation the Association became a parliamentary party called the Home Rule Party. In the general election following the introduction of the 'secret ballot' (1872) the Home Rule Party had fifty-nine MPs elected, including Pat Smyth and John Martin. But Mitchel remained unimpressed and was adamant that the only solution to government in Ireland lay not in Home Rule but in a sovereign independent parliament in Dublin free from all British interference.

In addition to his work in journalism Mitchel wrote a large number of literary articles under the pseudonym Professor Cornelius O Shaughnessy. About this time also (circa 1868), under contract to D&J Sadliers, a New York publishing company, Mitchel had published his *History of Ireland*. The book was a continuation of another volume of Irish history by Abbe McGeoghegan and it took in the period from the Treaty of Limerick (1691) up to 1851. Mitchel later explained that the book was completed in haste and regretted he hadn't devoted more time to the task. Biographer Louis Walsh would disagree and in his opinion, 'This is a book that needs no apology.' At the time of publication Mitchel's *History of Ireland* was perhaps a leader in its field but, with the passing of time and the rewriting of history, it has gone out of print.

James worked with his father on the *Irish Citizen* for nearly five years and this probably explains why Mitchel carried it on for so long. His father's health and failing eyesight had become major sources for concern and they were forced to abandon the newspaper in 1873. Circulation figures were very much on the decline and this has to have been a factor as well.

That summer, James Mitchel would suffer another crushing blow with the sudden death of his wife Elizabeth in giving birth to their first child. Their baby daughter – John Mitchel's first granddaughter – sadly did not survive. More untimely and tragic death visited on a family already beset by it. For James, who was only beginning to get some stability and normality into his life, the loss was devastating.

For Mitchel the grieving was compounded further. The loss of two young members of his family was heartbreaking, but to watch his only remaining son James endure such terrible anguish accelerated the decline in his own health. He became extremely feeble and withdrawn and, for a time, close friends believed he might be dying. Remarkably he did recover but it was a very slow process. The threatened tuberculosis had sadly become a reality and there was no known cure.

By the spring of 1874 he had regained some of his strength and, during his lengthy convalescence, he decided he would defy the British authorities and return to his native land. Friends tried in vain to dissuade him, pointing out that another term of imprisonment would undoubtedly kill him, but his mind was made up. The desire to see the laurels of Dromolane, and hear once again 'the voices of Ireland's winds and waters' would override any consideration for his own personal safety.

He might die in the attempt, but John Mitchel had lost none of that steely determination during his long illness. He had been sentenced by a British court to 'transportation beyond the seas for a term of fourteen years' and had served almost twenty six years of that sentence. A feeble but unbroken John Mitchel would return to Ireland prepared to confront his enemies one last time. No one would deny him that final, triumphant and glorious act of defiance.

## Chapter 18

# Mitchel Returns in Triumph

LATE IN JULY 1874, with his daughter Isobel and Doctor William Carroll, a friend from Philadelphia, John Mitchel landed in Queenstown, (now Cobh) Co. Cork after 26 years in exile. The authorities didn't attempt to arrest him, as transportation as a punishment had been abolished, and the Act of Parliament (1848) under which he had he had been convicted made no provision for escapees. He was allowed to move openly and received a hero's welcome everywhere he went. Of course much had changed during Mitchel's period in exile and the political landscape had altered vastly from the famine-stricken Ireland he had been forced to quit over a quarter of a century before. Sadly most of his former friends and political comrades had either died or left Ireland.

Francis Meagher rose to the rank of Brigadier-General in the Irish Brigade fighting with the North in the American Civil War. After the war he was appointed temporary state governor of Montana. Mysteriously he drowned in the River Missouri on 1st July, 1867. It is not certain that Meagher's death was an accident as believed at the time and there is a strong suspicion that he was in fact murdered. In 1913, a man called Miller confessed that he had murdered Meagher but later retracted his statement. Francis Meagher was only forty-three years old when he died.

William Smith O'Brien was able to return to Ireland after his unconditional pardon in 1856. He had earlier been released from Tasmania in 1854 on the condition that he did not return to Britain or Ireland. Possibly disillusioned, he played no further role in Irish politics and moved to Wales in 1864. He died in Bangor, North Wales, in June of that year, aged sixty. His remains were brought home to Ireland and interred in Rathronan in Co. Limerick

John Blake Dillon, died suddenly in Co. Kerry in September 1866. The amnesty allowed him to return to Ireland in 1855 and he was elected MP for Tipperary in 1865. One year later, aged fifty, Blake Dillon died of cholera. Mitchel was in Paris when he learned of his friend's death and in a letter to Blake Dillon's brother wrote: 'The death of John Dillon is a real and bitter sorrow to me. There were few men of his type in the world. He was all wrong about almost everything. Nevertheless he was better than most people who are all right.' It was a wonderfully unique epitaph.

James Fintan Lalor who had taken charge of the *Irish Felon*, successor to the *United Irishman*, was arrested in July 1848 on a similar charge to Mitchel. He was released in November because of ill health. Undeterred by earlier failure he continued to work organizing the people for a future rising. His health steadily deteriorated and he died in December 1849. He was forty two years of age at the time of his death.

Charles Gavan Duffy emigrated to Australia in 1855, quitting what he described as that 'blind and bitter land', to practice law. There he was persuaded to enter politics and became speaker of the Victoria Parliament from 1877 to 1880. He was also prime minister for a year (June '71 – June '72). In a strange twist of fate he received a knighthood from Queen Victoria in 1873 for his services to the British Empire. He is surely the only man in history to have been tried for treason and later knighted by the British monarch. He retired to the south of France in 1880 and took up writing again. Gavan Duffy died in Nice in February 1903, aged eighty-six.

Thomas D'Arcy McGee emigrated to Boston, after the failed rising in 1848 and worked in journalism. He later moved to Montreal, Canada where he entered politics and became a member of the Canadian House of Assembly. He denounced a threatened Fenian invasion of Canada and was assassinated on

7th April 1868. He was returning home from addressing a public meeting at 2.00am when he was gunned down at his front door by a young Fenian sympathiser. He was buried on his 43rd birthday.

Thomas Devin Reilly, Mitchel's most loyal disciple, had died suddenly in Washington twenty years previously (March, 1854), aged only twenty-nine. His short life was not without its sorrow, losing two of his three children in infancy and dying penniless. After his escape to America, Reilly continued as a journalist and became editor of the New York *Democratic Review*. Mitchel, in the few years he had known him in Dublin, came to regard him as a genuine personal friend. Reilly's forty-five page letter to him while he was exiled in Tasmania was something Mitchel and John Martin greatly treasured.

Fr. John Kenyon who, next to John Martin was Mitchel's closest friend, died in 1869. He was a man of exceptional intellect and shared Mitchel's strong dislike of O'Connell. The 'rebel priest' disliked O'Connell's son John even more. His death, five years previously, meant that Mitchel's premonition that all three Johns – Kenyon, Martin and Mitchel – would never again meet, was realised (last meeting in Paris, September 1866).

Terence Bellew McManus, Young Irelander, who like Mitchel was transported to Van Diemen's Land, died in San Francisco in January, 1861. He was aged thirty-seven. The Fenian Movement in America had his body exhumed later that year and arranged his funeral procession across America to Ireland. Despite Dublin Archbishop Paul Cullen's opposition to the funeral, over twenty thousand people marched through Dublin to Glasnevin Cemetery, on a wet Sunday in November. The funeral gave the Fenian cause its first real impetus and boosted recruitment into its ranks dramatically.

And what of John O'Connell, bitter opponent of Young Ireland and leader of Repeal after his father's departure? The association predictably collapsed under his inept leadership in a matter of months. O'Connell was to serve as an MP for twenty-five years before resigning to take up a government appointment in 1857. He died the following year at his home in Dun Laoghaire aged forty-seven.

To the new generation in Ireland Mitchel had become something of a living legend and his return to Ireland was the embodiment of that legend. For the authorities in Dublin Castle he was an acute embarrassment. Except for having a careful watch kept on him for a breach of the peace, the Castle, through its agents, did not move against him. For Mitchel himself the adulation was all too much and, if at all possible, he avoided such occasions of public acclaim.

After spending a few days in Dublin where he received a tumultuous reception, he moved north to Newry where he spent a considerable amount of his time. Isobel was the only one of the Mitchel children born in Tasmania and, as this was her first visit to Ireland, was thrilled to visit her ancestral home in Dromolane. There, among the hills and valleys and streams which had never left his memory, Mitchel regained some of his old zest for life. Isobel was constantly by her father's side as he strolled or was driven through the Co. Down countryside. They spent two happy months in Ireland before returning to New York in early autumn.

The visit to Ireland with Isobel had given Mitchel a new lease of life and in early February 1875, with his son James, he made his last sea voyage, again crossing the Atlantic to Ireland. His failing sight was a grave cause for concern but this wasn't going to deter the indomitable Mitchel. He had received a cablegram while at home in Fordham informing him that a number of his political associates in Ireland had nominated him as the Westminster Parliamentary candidate for a seat in Co. Tipperary. The position had been vacated by Colonel Charles White, an Irish Home Rule MP. Initially, Jenny was to accompany her husband but she gave way in favour of James as it was felt he would be more useful in the heat of an election battle.

When Mitchel departed New York for Cobh he was unaware that he was unopposed for the seat, so when he arrived on 17th February he was already the elected MP for Co. Tipperary. Close friends detected in Mitchel a feeling of disappointment then realised that he had come home anticipating a vigorous election campaign and felt somewhat cheated. For Mitchel it was a case of, if there is no contest there is no real victory. The manner of his election victory even seemed to have an adverse effect on him physically, and he now looked more exhausted and frail.

In the British Parliament the following day, Prime Minister Disraeli proposed a motion that, as Mitchel was adjudged guilty of felony and sentenced to fourteen years transportation and not having served his sentence in full, he could not be elected a member of the Westminster parliament. A lengthy debate followed where Disraeli's motion was vigorously challenged by Mitchel's parliamentary friends, practically all of them Home Rulers. It was however eventually carried by a comfortable government majority. Mitchel's election was declared void and a writ was issued calling for a second election to be held on 11th March. He was immediately renominated and on this occasion was opposed by Stephen Moore, a 'token' Conservative candidate from Clonmel.

Mitchel agreed to be a candidate on the strict condition that, if elected, he would not, on principle, enter the British House of Parliament. He also stressed that if his election was again declared void he would stand again and again so long as the electors of Tipperary wanted him. Although his health was rapidly deteriorating and he could no longer endure prolonged exertion of mind or body, the prospect of an election battle again raised his spirits. His message to the Tipperary electorate was simple: the only Home Rule he would approve was the sovereign independence of his country.

Mitchel's attitude towards the Home Rule Movement can be clearly deduced from a letter he wrote to P J Smyth in September 1874 while he was on his first visit to Ireland. Smyth was the

Home Rule MP for Westmeath and had invited Mitchel to stay with him while he was in Dublin. Mitchel's response was abrupt to say the least.

> I will be the guest of no Home Ruler in Dublin, not even with John Martin. In fact, I am savage against that helpless, driftless concern called 'Home Rule' and nearly as vicious against your simple Repeal.

It was hardly the reply Smyth might have expected from the man whose escape from Tasmania he had masterminded. Mitchel had once described Smyth as 'my rescuer and faithful friend'. To Mitchel's greater disappointment John Martin was also a Home Rule MP having been elected for the Co. Meath constituency.

Mitchel was probably unaware how active a number of Home Ruler MPs were in the campaign to have him elected. Blake Dillon's two sons, William and John, were also prominent and rarely left his side. On many occasions John Dillon had to read Mitchel's speeches for him so exhausted had he become. It should also be mentioned that the Home Rule Party did not put up a candidate despite the fact that the Charles White, who resigned the seat, was a member of their party. Many former members of the Fenian Movement also campaigned to have Mitchel elected so he was very much a popular unity candidate.

The Tories accused Mitchel of 'parole-breaking' in Tasmania and warned that, if elected, he would again be debarred. The electorate however declared their faith in Mitchel's principles and their approval of his actions and he won convincingly on a four to one majority, Mitchel receiving 3114 votes and Moore a mere 746. This time, victory was much sweeter. On the 12th March he received the news by telegram of his historic triumph. He was confined to bed in 'Dromolane House' where he had gone to be with his brother and sisters.

In a letter of thanks to the people of Tipperary he again reiterated his 'abstentionist' intent and affirmed that British parliamentary government of Ireland was maintained only by military might. He also wrote after his election victory:

> In offering myself to the electors of Tipperary I had nothing to go upon but my past life, and I take it that the chief part about my past life which recommended me to the people of Tipperary was that I had made no peace with England.... I wanted to offer to the people of that gallant county one more opportunity of telling the whole world what value they set on the verdicts of packed juries, what respect they have for the decision of the judges whom England hires to do her work in this country.

Feeble in mind and body, the John Mitchel of '48 was still alive and well, and as defiant as ever. He would never make his peace with England not while there was a breath in his tired body.

## Chapter 19

# Death of John Mitchel

> His last moments were calm and peaceful, in suggestive contrast to the excitement of his life. All the fierce passion which he avowed and felt is now at rest.
> —*Times*, 21st March 1875

ONLY A MATTER OF days after his election success, Mitchel became extremely ill and James was dispatched to New York to break the bad news to his mother and two sisters that he was unlikely to survive. Mitchel himself was not aware just how seriously ill he was, and with his brother William to look after him in 'Dromolane House', he believed there was no need for concern. One day, quite out of the blue, he inquired of his brother, 'Am I dying, William?' On receiving a non-committal response, he added, 'Because that would be a serious business for me.' That quirky sense of humour hadn't deserted him even in the 'serious business' of dying.

On the morning of 20th March he informed his brother that he was feeling much better and thought that he might rise later that day. He then fell into a doze and, with his younger brother still keeping watch, passed away peacefully. John Mitchel was only fifty-nine years old when he died but so much had been packed into that hectic lifetime that one could be forgiven for believing he had lived decades longer.

The *Times*, never a great fan of the inveterate rebel during his life, wrote more charitably in its obituary on the morning following his death:

> John Mitchel died this morning at 8 o'clock at Dromolane, near Newry... A short telegram received last night that he was

John Mitchel, last portrait 1875

dangerously ill and sinking fast, was the only intimation that his eventful life was so near the end, and the letter which he addressed to the electors of Tipperary, dated only on the 17th inst., retained so much of the originality and vigour which characterised his style and composition that few could have supposed that this was the last rally of his intellectual and physical energies before absolute prostration. His last moments were calm and peaceful, in suggestive contrast to the excitement of his life. All the fierce passion which he avowed and felt is now at rest.

Fate had at least been kind in death, as he departed this life at home in Ireland surrounded by friends and relatives. Sadly however, none of his immediate family was present. On 23rd March John Mitchel was buried in the 'Old Meeting House Green' off High Street in Newry, in the same tomb as his mother and father. It was Jenny's wish that he be buried in Newry and not in Glasnevin as many had wished. All creeds, classes and shades of political opinion were represented at his funeral and he was mourned as a national hero.

His boyhood friend and brother-in-law John Martin – he had married Mitchel's youngest sister Henrietta in 1868 – bore his loss badly. After the burial service he had to be helped into his carriage. Exactly six days later, Honest John Martin as he was popularly known throughout Ireland, died at 'Dromolane House' surrounded by the Mitchel family. Even his political opponents admitted that while they may have disagreed with John Martin, they always found him totally honest.

He was three years older than his 'brother felon' and confidant. John Martin's death was the final act in an enduring and remarkable friendship – a boyhood friendship which continued for half a century and spanned the globe. John Martin was laid to rest with his parents in the Church of Ireland Cemetery, in Donaghmore, Co. Down. His simple headstone bears the inscription:

> John Martin born 8th September 1812, died 29th March 1875. He lived for his country, suffered in her cause, pled for her wrongs and died beloved and lamented by every true hearted Irishman.

A fitting obituary which appeared in the New York *Irish World* on 8th April 1875 alludes to the uncanny circumstances and timing of Mitchel's death.

> John Mitchel died in victory. The rebel-patriot passed from the state amid the plaudits of the whole Irish race and to the chagrin and mortification of the British Government and to every truly loyal subject thereof. It was a magnificent ending. And in the accident, or miracle, that wafted Mitchel over to Ireland, and in the halo of glory that encircled him afterwards on the hills of Tipperary, we recognise a poetic justice which grandly supplemented his long and chequered career.

Mitchel's wife of 38 years, Jenny, received the news of her husband's death just as she was about to depart for Ireland. James was still en route to New York and his mother was informed earlier by cablegram that her husband was critically ill. For her, not being with him in Dromolane was the denial of her last hope. Jenny, who had always been loving and loyal, eloping with him at sixteen years of age, who had shared his triumphs and disappointments, who had grieved with him at the loss of Johnny, Billy, and Henrietta, was denied the consolation of being with her beloved John when he departed from her and from life.

On a visit to Newry some months after her husband's death, she erected a simple granite monument to mark the place where her heart lay buried. Mitchel's brother William advised her not to erect a Celtic cross as she would have wished, as this was a symbol of Catholic Ireland and might give offence to Protestant families with loved ones buried in the same cemetery. On the monument, included with her husband's name and dates, Jenny also had inscribed:

> After twenty seven years in exile for the sake of Ireland, he returned with honour to die among his own people.

Jenny Mitchel was supported for the rest of her life by generous Irish-Americans who donated the substantial sum of thirty thousand dollars to a fund in her name. She lived to the last day of the nineteenth century, passing away at her home in Bedford Park, New York, on the 31st December 1899. She was seventy nine years old. Jenny was truly an outstanding lady in her own right. A lady with strong principles, she possessed the highest qualities of mind and heart which made her to the very end of her life, devoted to the man she had chosen in her girlhood. Rebecca O'Conner's extensive biography of her is a worthy testament to an incredible life of loyalty, fortitude and dignity.

Pretty Jenny, as she was affectionately known, was destined to outlive her husband by some twenty-four years and survived all but two of her offspring, James and Minnie. (Isobel died in New York in 1880 leaving behind an infant son.) Jenny Mitchel is buried in Woodlawn Cemetery, in the Bronx and her Celtic cross dominates the large Mitchel family plot. At the foot of the cross a bronze plaque reads:

> Jane Verner Mitchel, wife of John Mitchel, Newry, Ireland.
> Died in her eightieth year. December 31st, 1899.

James, we are informed, included Verner in the inscription to show to the world that, though she had been a member of that staunchly Unionist family, she was proud to be married to the Irish patriot, John Mitchel.

## Chapter 20

# The Immortal Part of Him

> Even those who dissent from his opinions do not deny that they were dictated by the purest motives, that they were maintained with consummate ability, and vindicated with heroic fortitude.
>
> — *William Smith O' Brien.*

JOHN MITCHEL DIED WITH all his political hopes and dreams unfulfilled but he died as he had lived in a war of words with his country's enemies. Had he come home to renew, through the Tipperary election, his life-long battle with the British establishment or quite simply to see his native land before death, we will never know. What cannot be disputed is that it was an altogether appropriate ending that combined both and as stated in the New York *Irish World* obituary 'the rebel-patriot died in victory'.

Despite the fact that much of his own life was marred by tragedy he never grew disillusioned and remained committed to the cause of Irish Nationalism right to the end – 'an unrepentant rebel' to use a phrase of his own. It is ironic, that at the time of his death, he should be an elected member of a parliament he spent much of his life openly at war with. But the of-times migrant life of John Mitchel was filled with many similar ironic twists and turns.

When Mitchel died in 1875 Home Rule under Isaac Butt was the largest Irish party at Westminster. In the General Election of 1874 they had won sixty seats and Charles Stewart Parnell would shortly be elected MP for Co. Meath. (In a by-election Parnell won the parliamentary seat vacated by the death of Honest John Martin.) Although only twenty nine years of age when he entered parliament in 1875, Parnell was soon to become the most powerful figure in Irish politics. He enjoyed immense popularity with the people and succeeded Isaac Butt as party leader only four years after his election to parliament.

Parnell drew support to 'Home Rule' from all shades of Nationalist opinion including members of the Fenians but his demand for a toothless parliament in Dublin would not have satisfied the uncompromising Mitchel. Like Wolfe Tone and the United Irishmen, he wished to break all connections with England and wasn't interested in an Irish Parliament that would be subordinate to any imperial parliament at Westminster. The removal of the last vestige of British rule on Irish soil was Mitchel's avowed aim and his resolve didn't weaken with age.

To the end of his life he remained resolute in his belief that an English parliament would never grant Ireland sovereign nationhood by constitutional means alone. He was equally resolute in his contempt for that same parliament advocating 'abstentionism' from his very deathbed. With characteristic candour he attributed his election success in Tipperary to

> a county making a desperate protest against the whole system of pretended parliamentary government in Ireland.

British Government policy in Ireland, in Mitchel's view, was a complete sham and someone had to expose it. Whatever the cost might be, Mitchel was prepared to pay it. His politics were deeply rooted in the Famine and thirty years on he was neither prepared to forget nor forgive Britain, with all her colonial wealth, for her pretence in dealing with it. Mitchel was totally convinced that the Great Famine would not have happened if Britain had earnestly wished to keep the growing population in Ireland alive.

> And still fleets of ships were sailing with every tide, carrying Irish cattle and corn to England. (*Last Conquest*)

Again and again he returned in his writing to the Famine and his rage against England was no less intense with the passing of time. He identified with his starving people and the whole Famine experience took on an immensely personal significance. Mitchel wrote of the Famine in a way no one in his epoch or since has emulated. He certainly wrote emotively about what he saw around him – 'sights that will never wholly leave the eyes that beheld them' – but he wrote with feeling and compassion. There was a sincerity in all that he wrote about the suffering and misery he witnessed during those awful years of Famine.

Writing in his introduction to *Jail Journal* in 1854, Mitchel refers back in the most graphic terms to the desperate plight of his fellow countrymen when faced with the inevitability of death:

> Families, when all was eaten and no hope left, took their last look at the sun, built up their cottage doors that none might see them die nor hear their groans, and were found weeks afterwards skeletons on their own hearths.

The Great Famine was not the only catastrophic event in Mitchel's life. There was the equally calamitous American Civil War. Regrettably his passionately held views on the righteousness of the Confederacy Cause contributed directly to the death of two of his three sons. For his most ardent admirer, his espousal of that particular cause must be very difficult to reconcile with his outright support for the exploited and oppressed in his native land. The would-be emancipator of a people made servile in their own land had become a key apologist, some might even argue unashamed champion, for slavery in America. It seems an extraordinary contradiction in principle.

Mitchel seemingly did not perceive this as being in any way, inconsistent or anomalous. He was convinced that the Confederate Cause was just and morally defensible and remained as intransigent as ever years after the war had ended. Significantly in 1857, four years before the outbreak of war, in response to constant and informed criticism from friends both in Ireland and America, he wrote:

> I prefer the South in every sense. I do really believe its state of society to be more sound, more just than that of the North; and whatever measures the South calls for and truly needs to secure and establish itself, I advocate.

There is no doubting Mitchel's sincerity regarding his support for the South but his judgement on the morality of slavery in particular must be seriously questioned. It is worth pointing out that his position on this vital issue was shared by very few, if any, of his former 'Young Ireland' associates. Most Irish exiles in America aligned themselves with the North and the Union but Mitchel left the North to live in the South so strong were his convictions.

The deaths of Johnny and Billy in battle were devastating blows but he bore his loss stoically. Perhaps he did get a measure of solace from the belief that they died in 'that just and noble cause' but the question of whose cause was it still remains. Was it Mitchel's cause or his sons' cause, or was it sadly, neither? If we can possibly set aside the huge personal cost, we are still faced with that vitally important question. Was it for John Mitchel, at the end of the day, a case of embracing that one cause too many?

The death of his two sons was a personal matter and something he only shared privately with Jenny. The circumstances of young Willie's death in particular must have been a source of terrible anguish for Mitchel. There are very few recorded instances where he wrote or spoke about his sons' deaths publicly. A close friend in Richmond, Mrs. Anderson, wrote of him:

> He never posed as a martyr, never made any appeals for sympathy, never spoke of personal trials. Yet his countenance, when in repose, had the marks of deep personal suffering.

There can't have been a day passed when he didn't count the unspeakable cost of a cause which Mitchel reluctantly accepted, was not in truth their own.

Indeed he might have been better to heed the sound advice given to him by a friend, Congressman Alexander Stephens of Georgia, a couple of years before the Civil War had begun. 'Your problem, John Mitchel,' Stephens cautioned, 'is that you plunge into everything all the way.' There was no question of being half-in or fence-sitting for Mitchel – it was total commitment or none at all. Certainly, on an emotive issue like the rights and wrongs of slavery, he might have been better advised not to dive in head first, without first weighing up all the implications. But then he rarely sought or accepted advice no matter how well-intentioned or from what quarter, such was the depth of his self-belief.

There were times when he was even arrogant and dismissive towards those who offered advice and didn't share his extreme views on slavery. He went so far as inventing his own word for those 'do-gooders' who believed in the equality of black and white, labelling them derisively 'Benevolists'. The 'Benevolists' once extended the hand of friendship and invited Mitchel to come back to them. With typical brusqueness he replied, 'Come back to you! Why, when was I ever amongst you?' This type of superior, egotistical put down was a most effective component in the John Mitchel defence mechanism.

It is probably true to say that Mitchel wasn't an egalitarian at heart if we analyse his observations of his fellow convicts in *Jail Journal* (3rd February 1849). He had little sympathy with their plight and describes vividly how he personally would deal with offenders. The whole ideology that all men are created equal sadly wasn't a doctrine which Mitchel fully subscribed to. His direct appeal in the *Citizen* (1856) for his Irish/American readership to support the retention of black slavery rather than 'jeopardise the present freedom of a nation of white men' can only realistically be interpreted as the views of a 'white supremacist'.

There is no evidence that Mitchel ever had any doubts or misgivings on the slavery question. However, the moral dilemma for his legions of admirers will always rankle. Why did he choose, so soon after arriving in America, to come down so immutably on the side of the Confederates? His abhorrence of the North's progressive ideals may explain his support for the South's resistance to change but it doesn't shed any real light on his forthright endorsement of slavery.

John Mitchel was an extremely complex and volatile character, so much so that at times he often appeared to be at war with himself. It was a trait he seemed powerless to control or, more likely, failed to recognise in himself. To the very end of his life he was at war on some front or other. He remained a fearless advocate of the truth regardless of the price it might exact. He accepted nothing short of the absolute truth, and nothing should ever be allowed to replace, distort, or sully it in any way. Truth, for Mitchel, should neither be suppressed nor silenced for any reason. Above all, it should never be traded or compromised even for political expediency. Unfortunately, in politics as in history, there is often more than one version or interpretation of the truth but for Mitchel compromise was never the option.

He abhorred hypocrisy and all forms of political insincerity and cared little whom he offended. Mitchel would not be bought or silenced, a quality even his enemies were forced to begrudgingly recognise and admire. In a letter to a friend written in 1857 he states:

> To be sincere, that is to deal honestly with one's self and with all the world, seems to me the greatest of all qualities.

There is no question that Mitchel tried to live his life in accordance with this fundamental principle. For him it was almost set in stone. It ultimately cost him dearly but his sincerity and honesty were beyond reproach.

Lord Stanley's summing up of Mitchel and his associates on the staff of the *United Irishman* is worth re-quoting in part (House of Lords 1848):

> These men are honest; they are not the kind of men who make their patriotism the means of barter for place or pension. They are not to be bought off...

Principle and patriotism were simply non-negotiable. It was this strength of character which made Mitchel stand out – and often alone – among the leadership of Young Ireland.

In the final chapter in a remarkable life it would also single him out as the authentic initiator of 'abstentionism' from Westminster. In 1875, prior to his electoral victory in Tipperary, Mitchel declared that if elected, it was intention never to set foot in the British Parliament. It was for Mitchel a crucial point of principle and his final act of defiance. He resolutely refused to recognise the authority or legitimacy of the British Parliament in Ireland. Mitchel set the precedent, and 'abstentionism' would later become party policy for future generations of Irish republicans to the present day.

Mitchel had an impulsive nature, almost reckless at times, and as a rule rarely apologised if offence was taken. On the other hand he didn't allow a difference in opinion get in the way of a long standing friendship, Meagher, Blake Dillon and Smith O'Brien being obvious examples. However, he wasn't quite so forgiving in the cases of Daniel O'Connell and Charles Gavan Duffy or Mr. 'Give-in' Duffy as he latterly referred to him. Mitchel seemed to have a profound mistrust for O'Connell, and politically Duffy and Mitchel had gone their separate ways in 1847.

Mitchel's ruthless denigration of O'Connell in particular, long after he had departed political life and life itself, certainly lacked sensitivity but Mitchel remained unremorseful. Like most in Young Ireland he had become disenchanted at an early stage with O'Connell. This would shortly develop into a consuming mistrust motivated by frustration at O'Connell's failure to provide meaningful leadership. Perhaps the two protagonists – excluding their divergent political standpoints of course – were more alike than they cared to recognise.

As a direct consequence of his impulsiveness, Mitchel's life was unpredictable and unsettled. He was destined to spend almost two thirds of his adult life exiled on three separate continents. At times he seemed to uproot on a mere whim, without seriously considering the effects his actions might have on those dearest to him. Referring to his nomadic lifestyle with Jenny, he once wrote, 'Poor Jenny, she might as well have married a homeless Bedouin or wandering Tartar.' It was an adventurous, fragmented life, no question, but much of the uprooting was of his own volition. Circumstances dictated that he spent a lot of his life separated from his family but it was his choice to move the family to Knoxville in Tennessee, a decision which was ultimately to change the course of their lives.

Not only did Mitchel find it difficult to remain in one place for long he also found it hard to remain, for any length of time, within a political party or grouping. In the context of Irish nationalism, nothing seemed to ever claim his full allegiance, with perhaps one possible exception – his own *United Irishman*. It was solely his project, his initiative and he was in sole control. Its life span was brief but he poured himself into it like a man devil-possessed. His commitment to other publications may have been much longer but contained nothing near the same fiery passion.

John Mitchel was a highly intelligent man and surely knew his writing had him on a collision course with a much greater force but he remained completely unfazed. He even went so far as to goad his enemies, Lord Clarendon in particular, into coming to him. He must have been aware of the perilous situation in which he was placing himself but believed Britain's role in Ireland had to be exposed and opposed. If he was to be the catalyst needed to precipitate rebellion so be it. At his trial he claimed he acted 'under a strong sense of duty and did not repent anything'. He was equally assertive when he stated that he was merely commencing on a course which he believed in time, others would finish.

John Mitchel possessed a self-belief, bordering on infallibility, and, consequently, was never a great listener. It is doubtful if he was essentially a democrat, so strong was his self-belief and intolerance of those who didn't share his opinions. Addressing an audience in Cork while still active within the Confederation Clubs (1847), Mitchel conceded that he:

> long felt he belonged to a party of one member – a party whose basis of action is to think and act for itself – whose one fundamental truth is to speak its mind.

A matter of months after this frank admission he had parted company with the Confederation Clubs and many of his closest friends. The whole idea of collective decision-making had little appeal for the recusant Mitchel.

More than twenty years later he was as anti-authority as ever. In a letter to a friend, (circa 1870) he openly declared:

> It is my mission in life to get into trouble with every government and in every country.

The passing of time had done little to mellow the rebel spirit in him. Maybe there was something of the latent anarchist as well in that fiery Mitchel temperament. He certainly seemed to take great delight in provoking authority, even to the very last days of his life.

His politics was staunch Nationalism – a great love for Ireland matched, in his case, by an even greater hatred for England, or the power she wielded over Ireland. A matter of weeks before his arrest Mitchel wrote in the *United Irishman*:

> the English (or Famine system) must be abolished utterly – in farms and workshops, in town and country, abolished utterly.'

He shaped his life upon hatred of that power and pledged himself to smash it or be smashed by it. This intense hatred was fuelled, in the main, by England's Famine policy in Ireland. He once confessed to a friend:

> this hatred of the British system was something which I chiefly cherished and cultivated.

And in an attempt to analyse what motivated him to act and write as he did, Mitchel agreed that 'perhaps there was less of love in it than of hate.'

In the same letter to his Irish friend, he wrote candidly of, 'the misfortune, I and my children had, to be born in a country which suffered itself to be oppressed and humiliated by another.'

Is it the case that his innate pride prompted Mitchel to 'cultivate this hatred of the British system' more so than an innate love for Ireland? There certainly seems to be an undercurrent of resentment in this statement that he had 'the misfortune to be born in Ireland'. He seemed uncomfortable at times with his own Irishness and the 'sentiment that one cannot be thoroughly Irish without being Catholic' may have played on his mind as much as his daughter Henrietta's. (Ch. 15)

It wasn't only what Mitchel saw as England's deliberate extermination policy during the Famine which enraged him but the 'hypocritical protestations of benevolence' she portrayed to an ignorant and gullible outside world. In his Introductory to *Jail Journal* he opens on precisely this point:

> England has been left in possession not only of the Soil of Ireland, with all that lives and grows thereon, to her own use, but in possession of the world's ear also. She may pour into it what tale she will: and all mankind will believe her.

It wasn't England's charity that Ireland needed but the God-given right to hold on to sufficient food, produced on Irish soil, to feed her starving people – 'and for food Ireland craved in vain'. On this he was unambiguous and, if we accept the basic common sense of Mitchel's argument, then famine need never have happened. The 'act of God theory' as an explanation for the Famine certainly cut no ice with Mitchel.

The blame for famine in Ireland lay squarely at the feet of Britain and her 'population-control' policy. To paraphrase the words of Arthur Griffith from Chapter 4:

> in a land so lost to reason, should the voice of sanity have been deemed mad?

While he was halfway round the world and on his way into exile, there was to be yet another ironic twist in events in Mitchel's life. His former adversary Lord Clarendon wrote an extraordinary letter to Lord John Russell, the British Prime Minister. In the letter Clarendon vindicates Mitchel's view that Britain totally lacked the will to tackle the famine and had embarked upon a genocidal policy in Ireland. Clarendon's letter, dated 26th April, 1849, may have been more than three years too late and have fallen on deaf ears, but it confirmed absolutely what Mitchel preached.

The Lord Lieutenant somewhat belatedly conceded:

> I do not think there is another legislation in Europe that would disregard such suffering as exists in the west of Ireland or coldly persist in a policy of extermination.

Mitchel could scarcely have expressed it more forcefully himself. It was, of course, too little too late to save Mitchel's fate.

Mitchel would bring the 'Famine Debate' to an even higher and more ominous level. He argued that if Britain consciously chose not to consider Ireland as part of the *'United Kingdom'* in Ireland's hour of greatest need, then Britain could scarcely complain when Irish separatists did likewise. Implicit in this rationale lay for Mitchel, that justifiable call to arms.

> 'He was a rebel politically, and a rebel intellectually and spiritually – a rebel with his whole heart and soul against the whole British spirit of the age'

This is Mitchel's description of the Dublin poet James Clarence Mangan yet it could so aptly have been written about Mitchel himself – the angry Young Irelander who possessed, or was possessed by, an obsessive hatred for Britain. These two powerful emotions lie behind much of what Mitchel wrote and is the reason why his writings had so powerful an influence in the spread of Nationalism in his lifetime and, more significantly, helped inspire future generations. His writing particularly influenced the thinking of Arthur Griffith, and Pearse described him as 'Ireland's greatest literary figure writing in the English language'.

Mitchel's belief, expressed in the *Citizen*, that war is often a nobler state than peace would certainly strike a favourable chord with future Nationalists like Pearse. Mitchel propagated the 'blood-sacrifice' ideal primarily in the context of pre-Civil War America but it would be taken up by Irish Nationalists in the early 20th century.

## A Cause Too Many 149

Mitchel believed war purified and ennobled the soul of a nation and that the 19th century was poorer because it lacked a major war. He glorified war when he wrote in the *Citizen* in July 1854:

> Peace is sometimes beautiful but it is often ignoble, corrupt and ignominious. Not peace but war has called forth the grandest, finest, tenderest, most generous qualities of manhood and womanhood. What made America and breathed into her nostrils a fiery life? War

There can be little doubt that Mitchel's style of rhetoric and exaltation of war had a definite appeal for Pearse and other leaders in 1916.

John Mitchel spent a comparatively short time actively engaged in the Irish political scene and the Southern Confederacy Cause occupied much more of his time if not energy. He didn't become a major player until he joined the staff of the *Nation* in December 1845 and his involvement ended with his transportation in May 1848. In that short space of time he was to make an invaluable contribution. He greatly influenced the direction of Young Ireland and with his powerful writing, kept it firmly focused on its Nationalist aspirations during his time with the *Nation*. The long-term impact of his contribution was possibly more significant.

Mitchel eventually became alienated from others in the Young Ireland leadership with his refusal to renounce the use of force. This led to him distancing himself from the Confederation although he didn't formally resign. It was a conscious decision brought about by a firm belief that there was no other way. Many members of Young Ireland may not have agreed with him latterly, but they respected him as a sincere comrade, fellow patriot and uncompromising leader.

His good friend Smith O'Brien, while conceding that they in the Confederation Council did not always identify with Mitchel's opinions, they recognised that he wrote and acted out of the purest of motives. Following Mitchel's expulsion from Ireland, Smith O'Brien in his capacity as chairman of the Confederation, described him as

> a man deeply versed in his country's history who read in that history one continuous tale of perfidy and rapine.

O'Brien's statement continues and is a testimony to Mitchel's tenacity and courage. Writing of the horrors of Famine and the desolation which Mitchel saw all around him, O'Brien relates how Mitchel

> 'found that same curse of misrule blighting a land fitted by the hand of Nature for the enjoyment of unrivalled felicity. Saddened and stung by such reflections, he vowed that he would expel from his native soil this spirit of evil or perish in the attempt'.
> —*Council of the Irish Confederation's address to the Irish people on Mitchel's transportation, dated June 1848*

It is probably fair to say he wasn't the most pragmatic of the Young Irelanders if we recall his plea in 1848 to the man who had no gun. 'Let him sell his garment and buy one,' was the advice he proffered. Surely he may at times have lost touch with reality, but he was driven by an undying hatred of England which caused him to ignore the practicalities. This is not to say he was any less patriotic. He wasn't a romantic patriot in the mode of Thomas Davis or most of his fellow Young Irelanders but his patriotism lay more in his love for the Irish people.

Mitchel was more of a political controversialist or agitator than an orthodox politician. 'Mainstream' politics was all too disciplined and restrictive for someone of Mitchel's restless nature. He was however, a brilliant political analyst and journalist and his greatest achievements undoubtedly lay in his writing. Indeed, had he not been born into the despoiled, misgoverned Ireland of his day he would most likely have flourished as a writer or historian without equal in his time? One only has to read 'June in the Famine Year' or his beautiful reminiscence on autumn-time in Ireland from *Jail Journal* (13th

September '48) to find living proof of Mitchel's talent for lyrical, evocative prose.

It is therefore in his literary achievements, as much as in his political influence, that the spirit of John Mitchel lives in Ireland today. It is to both these qualities, that Thomas Carlyle, the Scottish-born writer, historian and contemporary of Mitchel alludes when he wrote over one hundred and fifty years ago:

> Irish Mitchel, poor fellow... I told him he would most likely be hanged, but I told him too, that they could not hang the immortal part of him.

Seamus McCall, biographer, says of Mitchel the writer:

> If he had been the advocate of a more fashionable cause, and his life and work had accordingly been better known, there would be no textbook, anthology or history of literature without some tribute to Mitchel as a stylist, or some example of his majestic prose – with its wit, its cold logic, its emotional torrent, its biting satire and its passionate feeling for Nature.

There is little doubt that had Mitchel lived a settled life in Ireland, working as a lawyer in Newry, and devoted his leisure time to writing, most, if not all of McCall's assertion would hold true. He had a powerful style of writing, a supreme command of the English language, a brilliant intellect and rapier wit. And of course he had perfected the potent art of polemic. Mitchel wrote courageously and at times outrageously, he wrote viciously and sensitively, he wrote prolifically and creatively but above all, he wrote passionately. Perhaps his supreme attribute lay simply in the fact that he wrote it as he saw it and as he felt it. His language, particularly on the slavery issue, may at times have been intemperate even repugnant to many, but he remained unapologetic.

Mitchel's raison d'etre was to write. Journalism and not law was his chosen profession. Other things may have temporarily occupied his attention, including two incursions into the world of farming, but he invariably returned to his true vocation. His prolific and proficient letter writing shouldn't go unmentioned either. Living the life of an exile, he was constantly in touch with friends across the world by letter. He debated with absent friends through his letters and here we often obtain a clearer insight into his innermost political thinking.

On the two occasions Mitchel was imprisoned it was his ability with the pen and not the steel, which landed him there. His ability to provoke others by his writing was the most striking of his personal qualities. It was a quality that he also delighted in and on occasion, used with devastating effect. His strength lay in the sheer potency of his language coupled with an amazing capacity for searing invective. It was precisely this raging power of expression that singled Mitchel out as the most complex and compelling of the Young Ireland leaders and possibly, the most underestimated Irish writer of the nineteenth century. Regrettably it was also the source of much personal misfortune and grief.

In his biography entitled *Irish Mitchel* (published 1938) Seamus McCall summarises the complexity of John Mitchel's character succinctly for us:

> John Mitchel was a man in whom the elements so mixed as to make his life well worthy to be known.

## Chapter 21

# Last of the Line

IN 1918 AN AMERICAN airman, on a solo flight in Louisiana, fell from his machine and was instantly killed. He had just completed his training and hoped shortly to join America's war effort in Europe. An official Government inquiry later found that the 'Jenny' which he had been flying was fitted with a defective safety belt. The airman's name was John Purroy Mitchel. He was the only son of Captain James Mitchel and grandson of John Mitchel. He was thirty-eight years old, married but childless and with his death the Mitchel male line ended. His father, Captain James Mitchel had remarried in 1875 and his second wife was Mary Purroy. She was a Catholic and, on her mother's side, a member of John Blake Dillon's family.

John Purroy Mitchel was brought up in the Catholic faith and it was something he cherished all his life. He was admitted to the New York Bar in 1901 when only twenty-one, having graduated from New York Law School. In 1914 he was elected mayor of New York for a three-year term receiving support from both Republicans and a number of disgruntled Democrats. Their hope was to restore honest and accountable administration to their city. The main opposition to change strangely came from Tammany Hall – a corrupt political group with strong Irish-Catholic origins. At the time Tammany Hall would have been closely aligned with the Democratic Party.

Mitchel, who was thirty-five years old at the time of his election and the youngest New York Mayor ever to hold the office, made no effort to curry favour with Tammany Hall. They, in turn, accused him of turning his back on his Irish roots and rising above his station. The young mayor regarded himself first and foremost an American citizen and secondly an Irishman. Like his grandfather before him, he was not afraid to air unpopular views regardless of whom they offended. His zealous campaign against corruption naturally brought him into conflict with those people he might have expected to support him including the Catholic Church.

The leader of the church in New York at that time was Cardinal John Murphy Farley, a native of Newtownhamilton in Co. Armagh. He was an out and out critic of Mitchel's mayoral policies, believing no secular body had the right to investigate Church matters even if they received public funding. Mitchel's education policy for the city was also proving unpopular with his co-religionists and the hierarchy. He favoured a form of vocational training rather than the traditional academic education for immigrant children. This was perceived by many as an unjust subterfuge to deny them upward mobility through the time-honoured professions. It was also deemed, on Mitchel's part, as a betrayal of his Irish origins and did little to enhance his popularity among the huge immigrant electorate.

When fresh elections were held in late 1917 John Purroy Mitchel was not surprisingly defeated. He had many of his grandfather's qualities and was not a man who would be bought. Unfortunately he had also rubbed too many influential people up the wrong way. Their combined force would ensure he didn't serve for a second term despite the fact that New York had prospered during his tenure of office. He had introduced many waste-cutting measures and accounting practices which earned the city national acclaim but this would not secure his re-election. His successor, John F Hylan, also of Irish Catholic ancestry, was a member of the Democratic Party and had strong Tammany Hall backing. Hylan won convincingly, in a bitterly fought election campaign.

When his mayoral duties ceased on 1st January 1918 John Mitchel immediately enlisted in the Signal Corps Army Air Service hoping to join the American forces engaged in the Great

War in Europe. His grandfather may have shifted uneasily in his grave in Newry but John Purroy Mitchel was always his own man and England's difficulty being Ireland's opportunity meant little to him. At the age of thirty-eight he had the rare distinction of being the oldest trainee pilot in the Air Service, an indication of the strength of public duty he felt.

A matter of weeks after completing his aviation training the Mitchel family suffered yet further tragedy when Major John Mitchel fell from his plane and died instantly. It was a sad end to a very promising life and many believed the highest office in the land was within his capabilities. He was thirteen days short of his 39th birthday when he died on 6th July 1918.

That section of the press which helped hound him out of office almost gloated at his death. They spuriously claimed that Mitchel couldn't face up to the public humiliation of his election defeat and chose suicide as the easy way out. All indications prior to his death were positive and upbeat and he was looking forward to serving his country in Europe. He had written to his mother only days before his accident expressing his eagerness to participate in what he saw as a righteous cause and his civil duty. The official government inquiry into his death quashed all allegations of suicide and a year after his death the military Airfield No. 2, based in Long Island, was named 'Mitchel Field' in his honour.

Cardinal Farley, in a dramatic change of heart, and recognizing the huge outpouring of grief among New Yorkers, insisted that the former mayor's Requiem be held in St. Patrick's Cathedral where he would officiate. It is recorded that upwards of one million citizens lined the streets of New York in moving tribute to the 'Boy Mayor'. His coffin was carried from the city's cathedral to the family plot in Woodlawn Cemetery by a foot parade. He lies at rest with his father and his grandmother Jenny Mitchel in the family vault. Among the many dignitaries present at what was believed to be the largest funeral ever seen in New York at the time, was former president, Theodore Roosevelt.

## 156  John Mitchel

John Purroy Mitchel's memorial, New York

At one of the entrances to New York's Central Park there is now a more than life-size gilt bust of John Purroy Mitchel. It was unveiled in 1926 and on the black surround the inscription includes:

> John Purroy Mitchel, Mayor of New York. Died in the service of the United States, July 6th 1918.

Although there is no monument erected to his illustrious grandfather in the United States, he does have the rare distinction of having a county named in his honour. Mitchell County (spelt with two lls), an area of approximately 500 square miles and with a population of 11,000 people is situated in the north east of the state of Iowa. Established in 1851, 'it is believed the statesmen of Iowa City bestowed the name in honour of that noble Irish patriot, John Mitchel' (*Chap. 4. History of Iowa* -1883).

In 1965, to commemorate the 150th anniversary of the birth of John Mitchel, a monument in his honour was finally raised in Ireland. Suitably it was in his home town of Newry and stands at the entrance to St. Colman's Park just off Hill Street. It is a fitting and impressive statue carved in local stone and stands on a granite plinth. The inscription on the plinth is similar to that which Jenny had carved on her husband's tombstone:

> John Mitchel 1815 - 1875. After twenty seven years in exile for the sake of Ireland, he returned with honour to die among his own people.

John Mitchel's statue, Newry

# Selected Bibliography

Boylan, Henry.1978, *Dictionary of Irish Biography*, Gill and Macmillan, Dublin.

Collins, M E. 1972, *Ireland Three*, The Educational Company of Ireland, Dublin.

Dillon, William. 1888, *Life of John Mitchel*, London Kegan Paul Trench and Company.

Griffith, Arthur. 1913, *Appendages to Jail Journal*, M.H.Gill and Son, Dublin

Holohan, P. 1973, *Ireland Two*, The Educational Company of Ireland, Dublin.

Jackson, Alvin. 1998, *Ireland 1798–1998*, Blackwell Publishers Limited, Oxford, England.

Kenny, Michael. 1994, *The Fenians*, Town House and Country House Publishers, Dublin.

Kinealy, Christine. 1994, *This Great Calamity: The Irish Famine 1845-1852*, Gill and Macmillan, Dublin.

Magazine Committee. 1975, *Benbradagh Issue No.5*, Dungiven Parish, Co. Derry.

Mitchel, John. 1913, *Jail Journal*, M.H.Gill and Son, Dublin. First published in the *Citizen*, New York, 14th January to 19th August, 1854.

Mitchel, John. 1868, *A History of Ireland*, D&J Sadliers, New York and Canada.

Mitchel, John. 1982, *Jail Journal*, Paperback version by University Press of Ireland, Dublin. Critical Introduction by Thomas Flanagan.

Mitchel, John. Circa 1860, *The Last Conquest of Ireland (Perhaps)*, R and T Washbourne Limited.

Mitchel, John. 1920, *An Apology for the British Government in Ireland*, M.H.Gill and Son, Dublin.

McCall, Seamus. 1938, *Irish Mitchel*, Thomas Nelson and Sons, London and Edinburgh.

McCartney, Donal. 1987, *The Dawning of Democracy: Ireland 1800-1870*, Helicon Limited, Dublin.

O'Conner, Rebecca. 1988, *Jenny Mitchel: Young Irelander*, O'Conner Trust, Dublin and Tuscan, Arizona, USA.

O'Hegarty, P S. 1917, *John Mitchel – An Appreciation*, Maunsel and Company, Dublin and London.

*Pears Cyclopedia 1995-1996* Edition, Editor Dr. Christopher Cook. Pelham Books Limited, London.

Pearse, P H. 1924, *Collected Works of P H Pearse*, Phoenix Publications, Dublin.

Poirteir, Cathal (Editor). 1995, *The Great Irish Famine*, Mercier Press, Dublin

Walsh, Louis J. 1934, *John Mitchel*, The Phoenix Publishing Company Ltd., Dublin and Belfast.

Woodham-Smith, Cecil. 1962, *The Great Hunger*, Hamish Hamilton Limited, London.

*History of Iowa* Reprinted and Published in 1975 by Klipto Printing Company, Manson City, Iowa, USA. First published in 1883 by Union Publishing Company, Springfield, Illinois.

### Newspapers associated with John Mitchel in Ireland and America:

The *Nation*, Dublin. 1845 – 1847.

The *United Irishman*, Dublin. 1848.

The *Citizen*, New York. 1854.

The *Southern Citizen*, Knoxville, Tennessee and Washington, DC. 1857 – 1859.

The *Irish Citizen*, New York. 1868 – 1872.